# OLYMPIAD WORKBOOK

## NATIONAL SCIENCE OLYMPIAD

AF417761

**01** Learning Objectives

**02** Multiple Choice Questions

**03** HOTS (Achievers Section)

**04** Model Test Paper

**05** Answer Keys and Solutions

**06** OMR Answer Sheet

# V&S PUBLISHERS

*Published by:*

# V&S PUBLISHERS

F-2/16, Ansari road, Daryaganj, New Delhi-110002
☎ 23240026, 23240027 • *Fax:* 011-23240028
✉ info@vspublishers.com • 🌐 www.vspublishers.com

**Online Brandstore: amazon.in/vspublishers**

**Regional Office : Hyderabad**
5-1-707/1, Brij Bhawan (Beside Central Bank of India Lane)
Bank Street, Koti, Hyderabad - 500 095
☎ 040-24737290
✉ vspublishershyd@gmail.com

**Follow us on:**   

**BUY OUR BOOKS FROM:** | AMAZON | | FLIPKART |

© **Copyright:** V&S PUBLISHERS
ISBN 978-81-977761-4-4
**New Edition**

# PUBLISHER'S NOTE

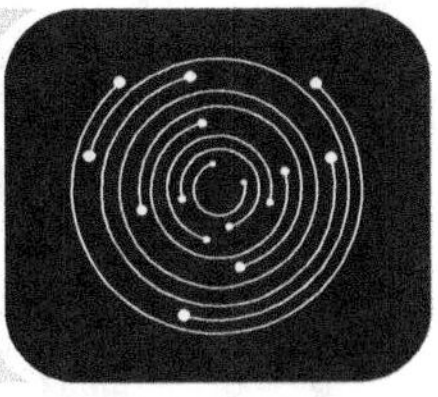

**V&S Publishers** has carved a significant niche in the publishing industry over the last decade, having successfully published more than 1000 titles across 9 languages spanning over 50 subject categories. Being known for the quality of content, we have built a reputation of excellence and reliability. We have consistently delivered **"Value & Substance"** to our readers, through a wide range of titles across a variety of genres covering school books, fiction and non-fiction that caters to different people from every section of the society.

The **Olympiad Guidebooks for classes 1-10** across all subjects, launched almost a decade ago, under the **GEN X Imprint**, became a go-to-source for the school students in no time, owing to their invaluable and substantive content written in a guidebook pattern,.

Having successfully sold a million copies of the same and in response to demand by both students as well as shopkeepers nationwide; we now present before you our newly launched **Olympiad Workbook Series**, designed for **classes 1-10 across 4 subjects**.

The workbooks are meticulously curated by a team of experienced educators, researchers and subject matter experts, edited by professionals and peer reviewed by teachers. The team has poured its efforts and expertise into creating a crisp and concise workbook which will help and guide the students to the path of success in Olympiad exams. The **MCQs** identified will not only help in scoring top marks in Olympiads but also inculcate a sense of deeper understanding of the subject, by way of solving **HOTS** and referring to complete solutions at the end of the book.

Here we present our new release– **OLYMPIAD WORKBOOK (NSO) CLASS–10** having following features:

☞ Based on the latest syllabi

☞ MCQs with comprehensive coverage of topics

☞ HOTS Questions liberally included

☞ A dedicated chapter on logical reasoning

☞ Model test paper for thorough practice

☞ Sample OMR sheet for real time simulation

We have made sure through our best efforts, that this workbook strictly follows the latest syllabi and patterns of the Olympiad Examination.

As **V&S Publishers** continuously strive to enhance the readability and maintain the credibility of our academic publications, we seek the support of our valuable readers in influencing and enriching the lives of future generations of students.

*P.S. While every care has been taken to ensure the correctness of the content, if you come across any error, howsoever minor, do not hesitate to discuss with teachers while pointing that out to us in no uncertain terms.*

We wish you all the best for your exams!

# DISTINCTIVE FEATURES



## 01 Learning Objectives

They list the whole chapter as subtopics, helping the teachers to guide children in a step-by-step manner.

## 02 Multiple Choice Questions

MCQs act as an excellent learning aid, helping you to understand and work on your mistakes.

## 03 HOTS (Achievers Section)

The High Order Thinking Questions aim to help the student to solve Application-based questions and gain practical understanding of the subject.

## 04 Model Test Paper

Model test paper are provided at the end of each book, which help the student to test the knowledge which they have gained after thorough reading of all chapters.

## 05 Answer Key

Detailed Answer Key along with explanations aid the pupil to indentify, understand the mistakes they make during the course of Olympiad preparation.

# CONTENTS

# CHEMICAL REACTIONS AND EQUATIONS

## LEARNING OBJECTIVES

➤ The characteristics of chemical reactions
➤ Chemical equations
➤ Various types of chemical reations
➤ The effects of oxidation in daily life

## MULTIPLE CHOICE QUESTIONS

1. When a black and white photographic film is exposed to light, the grey colour on the photographic film is due to presence of ___________.
   (A) $Ag_2O$
   (B) $Ag$
   (C) $Br_2$
   (D) All of these

2. Which of the following statements about the given reaction are correct?
   $$3Fe_{(s)} + 4H_2O_{(g)} \longrightarrow Fe_3O_4\ (s) + 4H_{2(g)}$$
   (i) Iron metal is getting oxidised.
   (ii) Water is getting reduced.
   (iii) Water is acting as reducing agent.
   (iv) Water is acting as oxidising agent.
   (A) (i), (ii) and (iii)
   (B) (iii) and (iv)
   (C) (i), (ii) and (iv)
   (D) (ii) and (iv)

3. Electrolysis of water is decomposition reaction. The mole ratio of hydrogen and oxygen gases liberated during electrolysis of water is ___________.
   (A) $1:1$
   (B) $2:1$
   (C) $4:1$
   (D) $1:2$

4. Which one of the following is an example of addition reaction?
   (A) $Cl_2 + 2\,KBr \longrightarrow 2\,KCl + Br_2$
   (B) $Fe + CuSO_4 \longrightarrow FeSO_4 + Cu$
   (C) $2\,H_2S + SO_2 \longrightarrow 2H_2O + 3S$
   (D) $CaO + H_2O \longrightarrow Ca\,(OH)_2$

5. The process of coating iron with zinc is called ___________.
   (A) Electroplating
   (B) Reduction
   (C) Polishing
   (D) Galvanisation

6. Which of the following gases can be used for storage of fresh sample of an oil for a long time?
   (A) Carbon dioxide or oxygen
   (B) Carbon dioxide or helium
   (C) Nitrogen or oxygen
   (D) Nitrogen or helium

7. The following reaction is used for the preparation of oxygen gas in the laboratory:
   $$2\,KClO_{3(s)} \xrightarrow[\text{Catalyst}]{\text{Heat}} 2KCl_{(s)} + 3O_{2(g)}$$
   Which of the following statement is correct about reaction for a decomposition reaction and endothermic in nature?
   (A) It is a decomposition reaction and accompanied by release of heat
   (B) It is a combination reaction
   (C) It is photochemical decomposition reaction and exothermic in nature
   (D) It is a decomposition reaction by absorbing heat energy.

8. Which of the following metal will react with dilute hydrochloric acid to give out hydrogen gas?
   (A) Cu
   (B) Pb
   (C) Ag
   (D) Hg

9. Which one of the following reaction will not take place?
   (A) $Zn + FeSO_4 \longrightarrow ZnSO_4 + Fe$
   (B) $Fe + NiSO_4 \longrightarrow FeSO_4 + Ni$
   (C) $2Al + 3MgSO_4 \longrightarrow Al_2(SO_4)_3 + 3Mg$
   (D) $Cu + 2AgNO_3 \longrightarrow Cu(NO_3)_2 + 2Ag$.

10. Rancidity is due to _____________.
    (A) Combination of oils and fats
    (B) Displacement of oils and fats
    (C) Oxidation of oils and fats
    (D) Reduction of oils and fats

11. Green coating on copper in rainy season is due to the formation of _____________.
    (A) $CuCO_3$
    (B) $Cu(OH)_2$
    (C) $CuCO_3.Cu(OH)_2$
    (D) $CuS$

12. Respiration is _____________.
    (A) An exothermic process
    (B) An endothermic process
    (C) Neither exothermic nor endothermic
    (D) Can be exothermic or endothermic

13. Which of the following are exothermic processes?
    (i)   Reaction of water with quick lime
    (ii)  Dilution of an acid
    (iii) Evaporation of water
    (iv)  Sublimation of camphor (crystals)
    (A) (i) and (ii)
    (B) (ii) and (iii)
    (C) (i) and (iv)
    (D) (iii) and (iv)

14. Which among the following is called double displacement reaction (s)?
    (i)  $Pb + CuCl_2 \longrightarrow PbCl_2 + Cu$
    (ii) $Na_2SO_4 + BaCl_2 \longrightarrow BaSO_4 + 2NaCl$

    (iii) $C + O_2 \longrightarrow CO_2$
    (iv)  $CH_4 + 2O_2 \longrightarrow CO_2 + 2H_2O$
    (A) (i) and (iv)
    (B) (ii) and (i)
    (C) (ii) only
    (D) (iii) and (iv)

15. A dilute ferrous sulphate solution was added to the beaker containing acidified permanganate solution. The light purple colour of the solution fades and finally disappears. Which of the following is the correct explanation for the observation?
    (A) $KMnO_4$ is an oxidising agent, it oxidises $FeSO_4$
    (B) $FeSO_4$ acts an oxidising agent and oxidises $KMnO_4$
    (C) $KMnO_4$ is an unstable compound and decomposes in presence of $FeSO_4$ to a colourless compound
    (D) The colour disappears due to the dilution: no reaction is involved

16. Which of the following is (are) on endothermic process(es)?
    (i)   Dilution of sulphuric acid
    (ii)  Sublimation of dry ice
    (iii) Condensation of water vapours
    (iv)  Evaporation of water
    (A) (i) and (ii)
    (B) (ii) and (iv)
    (C) (ii) only
    (D) (iii) only

17. Which of the following substance is reduced in the given reaction below?
    $$PbS_{(s)} + 4H_2O_2(aq) \longrightarrow PbSO_{4(s)} + 4H_2O$$
    (A) Lead sulphide
    (B) Hydrogen peroxide
    (C) Both lead sulphide and Hydrogen peroxide
    (D) Water

18. Which one of the following is not a chemical change?
    (A) Cooking of food
    (B) Evaporation of water

(C) Burning of candle wax

(D) Digestion of food in our body

19. Which one of the following solution on mixing will not form a precipitate?

(A) Lead acetate and potassium iodide

(B) Lead nitrate and sulphuric acid

(C) Iron sulphide and dilute sulphuric acid

(D) Potassium bromide and silver nitrate

20. Which one of the following on mixing with water will result in rise of temperature?

(A) Sodium chloride

(B) Sodium hydroxide

(C) Potassium nitrate

(D) $CuSO_4.5H_2O$

21. In which of the following chemical equations, the abbreviations represent the correct states of the reactants and products involved at reaction temperature?

(A) $2H_2(g) + O_2(l) \longrightarrow 2H_2O(l)$

(B) $2H_2(l) + O_2(l) \longrightarrow 2H_2O(g)$

(C) $2H_2(g) + O_2(g) \longrightarrow 2H_2O(g)$

(D) $2H_2(g) + O_2(g) \longrightarrow 2H_2O(l)$

22. Which one of the following does not result in the evolution of $H_2$ gas?

(A) Zinc and hydrochloric acid

(B) Iron and sulphuric acid

(C) Magnesium and very dilute nitric acid

(D) Aluminium and nitric acid

23. $Fe_2O_3 + 2Al \longrightarrow Al_2O_3 + 2Fe$

The above reaction is an example of a ____________.

(A) Combination reaction

(B) Double displacement reaction

(C) Displacement reaction

(D) Decomposition reaction

24. A balanced chemical equation is in accordance with which one of the following laws?

(A) Law of conservation of mass

(B) Law of conservation of energy

(C) Law of constant proportion

(D) Low of multiple proportion

25. Rust is ____________.

(A) $Fe_2O_3$

(B) $FeSO_4$

(C) $Fe_2O_3.xH_2O$

(D) $Fe_2O_3H_2O$

**HOTS (ACHIEVERS SECTION)**

26. Which of the following can undergo a chemical reaction?

(A) $MgSO_4 + Fe$

(B) $MgSO_4 + Pb$

(C) $ZnSO_4 + Fe$

(D) $CuSO_4 + Fe$

27. The reaction, $2C_2H_5OH + 2Na \rightarrow 2C_2H_5ONa + H_2$ suggests that ethanol is ____________.

(A) acidic in nature

(B) amphoteric

(C) basic in nature

(D) neutral

28. When sodium carbonate is added to acetic acid, $CO_2$ is produced. The other products of reaction are/is ____________.

(A) Sodium acetate and water

(B) Sodium acetate

(C) Water

(D) None of these

29. Which of the following statements is true?
   (A) In a combination reaction two or more substances combine to form a new single substance.
   (B) Two different atoms or groups of atoms (ions) are exchanged in double displacement reaction.
   (C) Decomposition reactions are opposite to combination reactions.
   (D) All of these

30. Reactions in which energy is absorbed are known as__________________________.
   (A) Exothermic reaction
   (B) Endothermic reaction
   (C) Redox reaction
   (D) Decomposition reaction



| 1. | Ⓐ Ⓑ Ⓒ Ⓓ | 7. | Ⓐ Ⓑ Ⓒ Ⓓ | 13. | Ⓐ Ⓑ Ⓒ Ⓓ | 19 | Ⓐ Ⓑ Ⓒ Ⓓ | 25. | Ⓐ Ⓑ Ⓒ Ⓓ |
| 2. | Ⓐ Ⓑ Ⓒ Ⓓ | 8. | Ⓐ Ⓑ Ⓒ Ⓓ | 14. | Ⓐ Ⓑ Ⓒ Ⓓ | 20. | Ⓐ Ⓑ Ⓒ Ⓓ | 26. | Ⓐ Ⓑ Ⓒ Ⓓ |
| 3. | Ⓐ Ⓑ Ⓒ Ⓓ | 9. | Ⓐ Ⓑ Ⓒ Ⓓ | 15. | Ⓐ Ⓑ Ⓒ Ⓓ | 21. | Ⓐ Ⓑ Ⓒ Ⓓ | 27. | Ⓐ Ⓑ Ⓒ Ⓓ |
| 4. | Ⓐ Ⓑ Ⓒ Ⓓ | 10. | Ⓐ Ⓑ Ⓒ Ⓓ | 16. | Ⓐ Ⓑ Ⓒ Ⓓ | 22. | Ⓐ Ⓑ Ⓒ Ⓓ | 28. | Ⓐ Ⓑ Ⓒ Ⓓ |
| 5. | Ⓐ Ⓑ Ⓒ Ⓓ | 11. | Ⓐ Ⓑ Ⓒ Ⓓ | 17. | Ⓐ Ⓑ Ⓒ Ⓓ | 23. | Ⓐ Ⓑ Ⓒ Ⓓ | 29. | Ⓐ Ⓑ Ⓒ Ⓓ |
| 6. | Ⓐ Ⓑ Ⓒ Ⓓ | 12. | Ⓐ Ⓑ Ⓒ Ⓓ | 18. | Ⓐ Ⓑ Ⓒ Ⓓ | 24. | Ⓐ Ⓑ Ⓒ Ⓓ | 30. | Ⓐ Ⓑ Ⓒ Ⓓ |

# ACIDS, BASES AND SALTS

## LEARNING OBJECTIVES

➤ Acids, bases and salts
➤ Indicators to identify acid and base
➤ The properties of acids and their uses

➤ The properties of salts and make use of the pH scale
➤ The role of pH in everyday life

## MULTIPLE CHOICE QUESTIONS

1. A salt on treatment with excess of ammonium hydroxide produces a complex tetraammine copper (II) ions. The salt contains __________.
   (A) Cuprous ions
   (B) Chloride ions
   (C) Cupric ions
   (D) Calcium ions

2. Which of the following phenomenon occur, when a small amount of acid is added to water?
   (i) Ionisation
   (ii) Neutralization
   (iii) Dilution
   (iv) Salt formation
   (A) (i) and (ii)
   (B) (ii) and (iii)
   (C) (iii) and (iv)
   (D) (i) and (iii)

3. What is pH of a solution whose hydrogen ion concentration is $1 \times 10^{-3}$ M?
   (A) 2
   (B) 3
   (C) –3
   (D) = 7

4. What will be pH of solution when 0.02 mole of hydrochloric acid in 2 litres of the solution?
   (A) 2
   (B) 1
   (C) –2
   (D) 10

5. When dilute hydrochloric acid is poured over powdered calcium carbonate, efflorescence is seen, because __________.
   (A) Acids are corrosive
   (B) Calcium oxide is formed
   (C) Carbon dioxide is evolved
   (D) Calcium carbonate is very reactive

6. Solutions A, B, C and D have pH 3, 4, 6 and 8. The solution with highest acidic strength is __________.
   (A) A
   (B) B
   (C) C
   (D) D

7. pH of two solutions A and B are 3 and 6 respectively. This means that __________.
   (A) Solution A is twice as acidic as B
   (B) Solution B is twice as acidic as A
   (C) Solution A is 1000 times more acidic than B
   (D) Solution B is 1000 times more acidic than A

8. In an attempt to demonstrate electrical conductivity through an electrolyte, the following apparatus was set up __________.

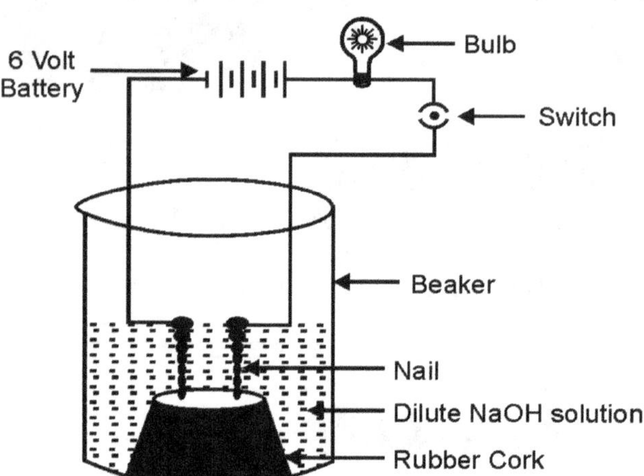


Which among the following statement(s) is (are) correct?

(i) Bulb will not glow because electrolyte is not acidic

(ii) Bulb will not glow because NaOH is a strong base and furnishes ions for conduction

(iii) Bulb will not glow because circuit is incomplete

(iv) Bulb will not glow because it depends upon the type of electrolytic solution

(A) (i) and (iii)
(B) (ii) and (iv)
(C) (ii) only
(D) (iv) Only

9. Which of the following substances will not give carbon dioxide on treatment with dilute acid?

(A) Lime
(B) Limestone
(C) Marble
(D) Baking soda

10. Which of the following is not a mineral acid?

(A) Hydrochloric acid
(B) Nitric acid
(C) Citric acid
(D) Sulphuric acid

11. Match the column A with column B and choose the correct option.

| Column A | Column B |
|---|---|
| A. Bleaching powder | (i) Preparation of glass |
| B. Baking soda | (ii) Production of $H_2$ and $Cl_2$ |
| C. Washing soda | (iii) Decolourisation |
| D. Sodium chloride | (iv) Antacid |

(A) A – (ii), B – (i), C – (iv), D – (iii)
(B) A – (iii), B – (iv), C – (i), D – (ii)
(C) A – (iii), B – (ii), C – (iv), D – (iii)
(D) A – (ii), B – (iv), C – (i), D – (iii)

12. Washing soda $(Na_2CO_3 \cdot 10H_2O)$ on exposure to air gives __________.

(A) $Na_2CO_3 \cdot 9H_2O$
(B) $Na_2CO_3 \cdot 7H_2O$
(C) $Na_2CO_3 \cdot 5H_2O$
(D) $Na_2CO_3 \cdot H_2O$

13. Aqueous solution of sodium carbonate is __________.

(A) Acidic
(B) Basic
(C) Neutral
(D) Amphoteric

14. Which of the following statements is not correct?

(A) All metal carbonates react with acid to give a salt, water and carbon dioxide

(B) Some metal react with acids to give salt, water and hydrogen

(C) All metal oxides react with water to give a salt and acid

(D) Some non-metal oxides react with water to form an acid

15. When hydrogen of an acid are partially neutralized by hydroxyl ion of a base we get __________.
    (A) Normal salt
    (B) Complex salt
    (C) Acidic salt
    (D) Basic salt

16. Which among the following is not a base?
    (A) NaOH
    (B) $NH_4OH$
    (C) $C_2H_5OH$
    (D) KOH

17. Which of the following is used for dissolution of gold?
    (A) Hydrochloric acid
    (B) Sulphuric acid
    (C) Nitric acid
    (D) Aqua regia

18. Plaster of Paris on mixing with water sets to form __________.
    (A) $CaSO_4 \cdot H_2O$
    (B) $CaSO_4 \cdot 1\frac{1}{2} H_2O$
    (C) $CaSO_4 \cdot 2H_2O$
    (D) $CaSO_4 \cdot 2\frac{1}{2} H_2O$

19. Match the column A with column B and choose the correct option.

| Column-A | Column-B |
|---|---|
| A. Plaster of Paris | (i) $Ca(OH)_2$ |
| B. Gypsum | (ii) $CaSO_4 \cdot \frac{1}{2} H_2O$ |
| C. Bleaching Powder | (iii) $CaSO_4 \cdot 2H_2O$ |
| D. Slaked lime | (iv) $CaOCl_2$ |

    (A) A → (ii), B → (iii), C → (iv), D → (i)
    (B) A → (iii), B → (ii), C → (i), D → (iv)
    (C) A → (ii), B → (iv), C → (i), D → (iv)
    (D) A → (i), B → (iv), C → (ii), D → (iii)

20. Common salt besides being used in kitchen can also be used as the raw material for making:
    (i) Washing soda
    (ii) Bleaching powder
    (iii) Baking soda
    (iv) Slaked lime
    (A) (i) and (ii)
    (B) (i) and (iii)
    (C) (i), (ii) and (iii)
    (D) (i), (iii) and (iv)

21. Equal volumes of solutions with pH = 4 and pH = 10 are mixed. What is the pH of the resulting solution?
    (A) 4      (B) 10
    (C) 7      (D) 14

22. The water of crystallization of green vitriol is __________.
    (A) 10      (B) 9
    (C) 7      (D) 5

23. A solution when reacts with zinc material liberates a gas which burn with a pop sound. The pH of the solution is __________.
    (A) Equal to 7
    (B) Greater than 7
    (C) Less than 7
    (D) Between 8 and 14

24. Glauber's salt is __________.
    (A) Sodium sulphate
    (B) Sodium sulphate decahydrate
    (C) Sodium carbonate decahydrate
    (D) Sodium carbonate monohydrate

25. The acid used for washing eyes is __________.
    (A) Boric acid
    (B) Acetic acid
    (C) Oxalic acid
    (D) Carbonic acid

26. Match the entries of column I with appropriate entries of column II and III

| Column I (Salt) | Column II (Nature of solution) | Column III (pH) |
|---|---|---|
| (i) Common salt | (A) Acidic | (A) < 7 |
| (ii) Blue vitriol | (B) Basic | (B) > 7 |
| (iii) Baking soda | (C) Neutral | (C) = 7 |
| (iv) Soda ash | | |

(A) (i) → (A) → (A), (ii) → (B) → (B), (iii) → (B) → (B), (iv) → (C) → (C)
(B) (i) → (C) → (C), (ii) → (C) → (C), (iii) → (A) → (A), (iv) → (B) → (B)
(C) (i) → (C) → (C), (ii) → (A) → (A), (iii) → (B) → (B), (iv) → (B) → (B)
(D) None of these

27. Calcium phosphate is present in tooth enamel. Its nature is ___________.
(A) Acidic
(B) Basic
(C) Neutral
(D) Amphoteric

28. What happens when a solution of an acid is mixed with a solution of a base in a test tube?

(i) The temperature of the solution increases
(ii) The temperature of the solution decreases
(iii) The temperature of the solution remains the same
(iv) Salt formation takes place
(A) (i) only
(B) (i) and (iii)
(C) (ii) and (iii)
(D) (i) and (iv)

29. Which of the following gives the correct increasing order of acid strength?
(A) Acetic acid < water < Hydrochloric acid
(B) Hydrochloric acid < Water < Acetic acid
(C) Water < Acetic acid < Hydrochloric acid
(D) Water < Hydrochloric acid < Acetic acid

30. A sample of soil is mixed with water and allowed to settle. The clear supernatant solution turns the pH paper yellowish – orange. Which of the following would change the colour of this pH paper to greenish blue ___________.
(A) Common salt
(B) Vinegar
(C) An antacid
(D) Lemmon juice

HOTS (ACHIEVERS SECTION)

31. pH of Ammonium chloride, $(NH_4Cl)$ and copper sulphate $(CuSO_4)$ solution will be ___________.
(A) 7
(B) > 7
(C) < 7
(D) O

32. When hydrogen chloride gas is prepared on a humid day, the gas is usually passed through the guard tube containing calcium chloride. The role of calcium chloride taken in the guard tube is to
(A) absorb the evolved gas
(B) moisten the gas
(C) absorb moisture from the gas
(D) absorb $Cl^-$ ions from the evolved gas

33. What is formed when zinc reacts with sodium hydroxide?
   (A) Zinc hydroxide and sodium
   (B) Sodium zincate and hydrogen gas
   (C) Sodium zinc-oxide and hydrogen gas
   (D) Sodium zincate and water

34. Which of the following statements is correct about an aqueous solution of an acid and of a base?
   (i) Higher the pH, stronger the acid
   (ii) Higher the pH, weaker the acid
   (in) Lower the pH, stronger the base
   (iv) Lower the pH, weaker the base

   (A) (i) and (iii)      (B) (ii) and (iii)
   (C) (i) and (iv)       (D) (ii) and (iv)

35. What happens when a solution of an acid is mixed with a solution of a base in a test tube?
   (i) The temperature of the solution increases
   (ii) The temperature of the solution decreases
   (iii) The temperature of the solution remains the same
   (iv) Salt formation takes place.
   (A) (i) only          (B) (i) and (iii)
   (C) (ii) and (iii)    (D) (i) and (iv)

# METALS AND NON-METALS

## LEARNING OBJECTIVES

➤ Metals, non-metals and metalloids
➤ Physical and chemical properties of metals and non-metals
➤ The importance of metals and non-metals

## MULTIPLE CHOICE QUESTIONS

1. Cinnabar is an ore of _____________.
   (A) Calcium      (B) Zinc
   (C) Mercury      (D) Copper

2. Safety fuse wire is made of _____________.
   (A) Platinum
   (B) Silver
   (C) Copper
   (D) Alloy of tin and lead

3. All ores are minerals but all mineral are not _____________.
   (A) Compounds      (B) Suspensions
   (C) Ores      (D) Mixtures

4. When aluminium is added to sodium hydroxide solution _____________.
   (A) Oxygen is evolved
   (B) Hydrogen is produced
   (C) Water is produced
   (D) No reaction takes place

5. The correct order of electrical conductivity is _____________.
   (A) Al > Cu > Au > Ag
   (B) Ag > Cu > Au > Al
   (C) Cu > Ag > Al > Au
   (D) Au > Ag > Al > Cu

6. Which of the following metals forms amphoteric oxide?
   (A) Copper      (B) Silver
   (C) Aluminium      (D) Iron

7. Beakers A, B and C contain zinc sulphate, silver nitrate and iron (II) sulphate solutions, respectively, copper pieces are added to each beaker. Blue colour will appear in case of _____________.
   (A) Beaker A
   (B) Beaker B
   (C) Beaker C
   (D) All the beakers

8. Match the entries of column I with appropriate entries of column II and choose the correct option.

| Column I (Metal) | Column II (Ore of Metal) |
|---|---|
| (i) Aluminium | (A) Calamine |
| (ii) Iron | (B) Dolomite |
| (iii) Lead | (C) Cinnabar |
| (iv) Mercury | (D) Haematite |
| (v) Zinc | (E) Galena |
| (vi) Calcium | (F) Bauxite |



OLYMPIAD WORKBOOK (NSO) CLASS— 10

(A) (i) $\to$ F, (ii) $\to$ D, (iii) $\to$ (E), (iv) $\to$ (C), (v) $\to$ A, (vi) $\to$ (B)

(B) (i) $\to$ D, (ii) $\to$ A, (iii) $\to$ (B), (iv) $\to$ (E), (v) $\to$ F, (vi) $\to$ (C)

(C) (i) $\to$ B, (ii) $\to$ C, (iii) $\to$ (E), (iv) $\to$ (A), (v) $\to$ D, (vi) $\to$ (F)

(D) (i) $\to$ C, (ii) $\to$ D, (iii) $\to$ (A), (iv) $\to$ (B), (v) $\to$ F, (vi) $\to$ (E)

9. Which of the following oxides cannot be reduced with carbon to obtain the metal?

(A) $MnO_2$      (B) $Al_2O_3$

(C) $Cr_2O_3$      (D) All of these

10. 18 carat gold contains __________.

(A) 5% gold      (B) 75% gold

(C) 18% gold      (D) 60% gold

11. Which of the following is not ionic compounds?

(i) KCl      (ii) HCl

(iii) $CCl_4$      (iv) NaCl

(A) (i) and (ii)      (B) (ii) and (iii)

(C) (iii) and (iv)      (D) (i) and (iii)

12. The composition of aqua regia is __________.

(A) Dil HCl : Conc $HNO_3$    3    1

(B) Conc HCl : Dil $HNO_3$    3 : 1

(C) Conc HCl : Conc $HNO_3$    3 : 1

(D) Dil HCl : Dil $HNO_3$    3 : 1

13. What happens when calcium is treated with water?

(i) It does not react with water

(ii) It reacts violently with water

(iii) It reacts less violently with water

(iv) Bubbles of hydrogen gas formed stick to the surface of calcium

(A) (i) and (iv)

(B) (ii) and (iii)

(C) (iii) and (iv)

(D) (i) and (ii)

14. Which one of the following metals does not react with cold as well as hot water?

(A) Na      (B) Mg

(C) Ca      (D) Fe

15. Generally metals react with acids to give salt and hydrogen gas. Which of the following acids does not give hydrogen gas on reacting with metals (except Mn and Mg)?

(A) HCl      (B) $H_2SO_4$

(C) $HNO_3$      (D) All of these

16. Which one of the following four metals would be displaced from the solution of its salts by other three metals?

(A) Ag      (B) Cu

(C) Mg      (D) Zn

17. An alloy is __________.

(A) An element

(B) A compound

(C) A homogeneous mixture

(D) A heterogeneous mixture

18. Which of the following oxide(s) of iron would be obtained on prolonged reaction of iron with steam?

(A) FeO

(B) $Fe_2O_3$

(C) $Fe_3O_4$

(D) $Fe_2O_3$ and $Fe_3O_4$

19. The most abundant metal on the earth's crust is __________.

(A) Copper      (B) Zinc

(C) Aluminium      (D) Iron

20. When a sample of copper containing iron as impurity is purified by electrolysis, the appropriate electrodes taken as cathode and anode are __________.

(A) Pure iron pure copper

(B) Impure sample pure copper

(C) Impure iron impure sample

(D) Pure copper impure sample

21. Which of the following metals exist in their native state?
   (i) Cu
   (ii) Au
   (iii) Zn
   (iv) Ag
   (A) (ii) and (iv)
   (B) (i) and (iii)
   (C) (iii) and (iv)
   (D) (ii) and (iii)

22. Match the entries of column I with entries of column II and choose the correct option.

| Column-I (Metal and its Ore) | Column-II (Method of Concentration) |
| --- | --- |
| (i) Iron from haematite | (A) Froth floation |
| (ii) Copper from copper glance | (B) Gravity separation |
| (iii) Aluminium from bauxite | (C) Chemical separation |
| (iv) Chromium from chromite ore | (D) Hydraulic washing |

   (A) (i)→(B), (ii)→(A), (iii)→(D), (iv)→(C)
   (B) (i)→(C), (ii)→(D), (iii)→(A), (iv)→(B)
   (C) (i)→(D), (ii)→(A), (iii)→(C), (iv)→(B)
   (D) (i)→(B), (ii)→(C), (iii)→(D), (iv)→(A)

23. Silver articles become black on prolonged exposure to air. This is due to the formation __________.
   (A) $Ag_3N$
   (B) $Ag_2S$
   (C) $Ag_2O$
   (D) $Ag_2S$ and $Ag_3N$

24. Galvanization is a method of protecting iron from rusting by coating with thin layer of __________.
   (A) Zinc
   (B) Silver
   (C) Galium
   (D) Aluminium

25. If copper is kept open in air, it slowly losses its shining brown surface and gains a green coating. It is due to the formation of __________.
   (A) $CuO$
   (B) $CuSO_4$
   (C) $CuCO_3$
   (D) $Cu(NO_3)_2$

26. Which of the following metals are obtained by electrolysis of their chloride in molten state?
   (i) Na
   (ii) Ca
   (iii) Fe
   (iv) Cu
   (A) (i) and (iv)
   (B) (i) and (ii)
   (C) (i) and (iii)
   (D) (iii) and (iv)

27. During electrolytic refining of zinc, it gets __________.
   (A) Deposited on anode
   (B) Deposited on cathode
   (C) Deposited on cathode as well as anode
   (D) Remains in the solution

28. An element A is soft and can be cut with a knife. This is very reactive to air and cannot to kept open in air. It reacts vigorously with water. Identify the element from the following __________.
   (A) Ca
   (B) P
   (C) Na
   (D) Mg
   (e) Fe

29. An electrolytic cell consists of __________.
   (i) Positively charged cathode
   (ii) Negatively charged anode
   (iii) Positively charged anode
   (iv) Negatively charged cathode
   (A) (i) and (ii)
   (B) (i) and (iii)
   (C) (ii) and (iii)
   (D) (iii) and (iv)

30. Generally, metals are solid in nature. Which one of the following metals is found in liquid state at room temperature?
   (A) Na
   (B) Cr
   (C) Hg
   (D) Fe

31. Two ml each of concentrated HCl, $HNO_3$ and a mixture of concentrated HCl and concentrated $HNO_3$ in the ratio of 3 : 1 were taken in three test tubes labelled as A, B and C. A small piece of metal was put in each test tube. No change occurred in test tubes A and B but the metal got dissolved in test tube C. The metal could be ____________.
    (A) Au                    (B) Al
    (C) Pt                    (D) Cu

32. Reaction between X and Y forms compound Z. X loses electron and Y gains electron. Which of the following properties is not shown by Z?
    (A) Has low melting point
    (B) Has high melting point
    (C) Occurs as solid
    (D) Conducts electricity in molten state

33. The electronic configuration of three elements X, Y and Z are X−2, 8; Y−2, 8, 7 and Z−2, 8, 2 which of the following is correct?
    (A) X is metal
    (B) Y is a metal
    (C) Z is a non-metal
    (D) Y is a non-metal and Z is a metal

34. Although metals form basic oxides, which of the following metals forms an amphoteric oxide?
    (A) Na                    (B) Cu
    (C) Ca                    (D) Al

35. 18 carat gold contains ____________.
    (A) 50% gold              (B) 18% gold
    (C) 75% gold              (D) 60% gold

—Darken Your Choice with HB Pencil—

| 1. | (A) (B) (C) (D) | 8. | (A) (B) (C) (D) | 15. | (A) (B) (C) (D) | 22 | (A) (B) (C) (D) | 29. | (A) (B) (C) (D) |
|---|---|---|---|---|---|---|---|---|---|
| 2. | (A) (B) (C) (D) | 9. | (A) (B) (C) (D) | 16. | (A) (B) (C) (D) | 23. | (A) (B) (C) (D) | 30. | (A) (B) (C) (D) |
| 3. | (A) (B) (C) (D) | 10. | (A) (B) (C) (D) | 17. | (A) (B) (C) (D) | 24. | (A) (B) (C) (D) | 31. | (A) (B) (C) (D) |
| 4. | (A) (B) (C) (D) | 11. | (A) (B) (C) (D) | 18. | (A) (B) (C) (D) | 25. | (A) (B) (C) (D) | 32. | (A) (B) (C) (D) |
| 5. | (A) (B) (C) (D) | 12. | (A) (B) (C) (D) | 19. | (A) (B) (C) (D) | 26. | (A) (B) (C) (D) | 33. | (A) (B) (C) (D) |
| 6. | (A) (B) (C) (D) | 13. | (A) (B) (C) (D) | 20. | (A) (B) (C) (D) | 27. | (A) (B) (C) (D) | 34. | (A) (B) (C) (D) |
| 7. | (A) (B) (C) (D) | 14. | (A) (B) (C) (D) | 21. | (A) (B) (C) (D) | 28. | (A) (B) (C) (D) | 35. | (A) (B) (C) (D) |

# CARBON AND ITS COMPOUND 

**4**

## LEARNING OBJECTIVES

➤ Covalent bonding in carbon compounds
➤ Allotropic forms of carbon
➤ Vital force theory and Wohler's synthesis

## MULTIPLE CHOICE QUESTIONS

1. Functional groups present in aspirin are ____________ .

The structure shows a benzene ring with an $-O-C(=O)-CH_3$ (ester) group and a $HO-C(=O)-$ (carboxylic acid) group.

   (A) Ester and aldehyde
   (B) Ester and carboxylic acid
   (C) Easter and ketone
   (D) Carboxylic acid and ether

2. Which one of the following is a functional group of alcohol?
   (A) $R - OH$      (B) $R - COOH$
   (C) $R - CO - R$      (D) $R - CHO$

3. The reaction $2C_2H_5OH + 2Na \longrightarrow 2C_2H_5ONa + H_2$ suggests that ethanol is ____________ .
   (A) Acidic in nature    (B) Amphoteric
   (C) Neutral      (D) Basic in nature

4. $CH_3-CH_2-OH \xrightarrow[\text{Heat}]{\text{Alkaline kMnO}_4} CH_3-COOH$

   In the above reaction, alkaline $kMnO_4$ acts as ____________ .
   (A) Catalyst
   (B) Reducing agent
   (C) Oxidising agent
   (D) Dehydrating agent

5. Buckminster fullerene is an allotropic form of ____________ .
   (A) Phosphorus
   (B) Sulphur
   (C) Carbon
   (D) Tin

6. Which of the following is the correct representation of electron dot structures of nitrogen?
   (A) $:\dot{N}::\dot{N}:$      (B) $\dot{N}::\dot{N}$
   (C) $:\dot{N}:\dot{N}:$      (D) $:\dot{N}:N:$

7. Which of the following represents an esterfication reaction?
   (A) $CH_4 + Cl_2 \longrightarrow CH_3Cl + HCl$
   (B) $CH_3COOC_2H_5 + NaOH \xrightarrow{\text{Heat}} CH_3COONa + C_2H_5OH$
   (C) $CH_3COONa + NaOH \xrightarrow{\text{CaO 633 K}} CH_4 + Na_2CO3$
   (D) $CH_3COOH + C_2H_5OH \xrightarrow{\text{Conc. H}_2SO_4} CH_3COOC_2H_5 + H_2O$

8. Which of the following substances is added to denature ethanol?
   (A) Methanol
   (B) Copper sulphate
   (C) Pyridine
   (D) All of these

9. Oils on treating with hydrogen in the presence of palladium or nickel catalyst form fats. This is an example of ___________.
   (A) Oxidation reaction
   (B) Displacement reaction
   (C) Addition reaction
   (D) Substitution reaction

10. A molecule of ammonia ($NH_3$) has ___________.
    (A) Only single bond
    (B) Only double bonds
    (C) Only triple bonds
    (D) Two double bonds and one single bond

11. The first member of alkyne homologus series is ___________.
    (A) Ethyne          (B) Ethene
    (C) methane         (D) ethane

12. Carbon forms four covalent bonds by sharing its four valence electrons with four univalent atoms, e.g., hydrogen. After the formation of four bonds, carbon attains the electronic configuration of ___________.
    (A) Helium          (B) Neon
    (C) Krypton         (D) Argon

14. Which of the following set of compounds have the same molecular formula?
    (A) Butane and isobutane
    (B) Cyclohexane and 1-hexen
    (C) Both of these
    (D) None of these

15. While cooking if the bottom of the vessel is getting blackened on the outside. It means that ___________.
    (A) The food is not cooked completely
    (B) The fuel is wet
    (C) The fuel is burning completely
    (D) The fuel is not burning completely

16. Which of the following substance cannot be used to distinguish ethanol from ethanoic acid?
    (A) $NaHCO_3$
    (B) Hot alkaline $KMnO_4$ solution
    (C) Na metal
    (D) Hot acidified $K_2Cr_2O_7$ solution

17. Vinegar is a solution of ___________.
    (A) 50%–60% acetic acid and in water
    (B) 50%–60% acetic acid in alcohol
    (C) 5%–8% acetic acid in water
    (D) 5%–8% acetic acid in alcohol

18. Rubbing alcohol is ___________.
    (A) $CH_3OH$
    (B) $C_2H_5OH$
    (C) $C_3H_7OH$
    (D) $C_5H_{11}OH$

13. Match the reactions given in column (A) with the names given in column (B).

| Column A | Column B |
| --- | --- |
| (A) $CH_3OH + CH_3COOH \xrightarrow{H^+} CH_3COOCH_3 + H_2O$ | (i) Addition reaction |
| (B) $CH_2 = CH_2 + H_2 \xrightarrow{Ni} CH_3 - CH_3$ | (ii) Substitution reaction |
| (C) $CH_4 + Cl_2 \xrightarrow{Sunlight} CH_3Cl + HCl$ | (iii) Neutralisation reaction |
| (D) $CH_3COOH + NaOH \longrightarrow CH_3COONa + H_2O$ | (iv) Esterification reaction |

   (A) A – (ii), B – (i), C – (iv), D – (iii)      (B) A – (iv), B – (i), C – (ii), D – (iii)
   (C) A – (iii), B – (ii), C – (i), D – (ii)      (D) A – (iv), B – (iii), C – (iv), D – (i)

19. The correct electron dot structure of a water molecule is ______________.

(A) $H \cdot \ddot{O} \cdot H$

(B) $H : \ddot{O} \cdot H$

(C) $H \cdot \ddot{O} : H$

(D) $H : \ddot{O} : H$

20. The soap molecule has a ______________.

(A) Hydrophilic head and a hydrophilic tail

(B) Hydrophilic head and a hydrophobic tail

(C) Hydrophobic head and a hydrophobic tail

(D) Hydrophobic head and a hydrophilic tail

21. The correct structural formula of butanoic acid is ______________.

(A)
```
      H   H   O
      |   |   ||
  H - C - C = C - C - OH
      |
      H
```

(B)
```
      H   H   H   O
      |   |   |   ||
  H - C - C - C - C - OH
      |   |   |
      H   H   H
```

(C)
```
      H   H   H   H   O
      |   |   |   |   ||
  H - C - C - C - C - C - OH
      |   |   |   |   |
      H   H   H   H   H
```

(D)
```
      H   H   H   H
      |   |   |   |
  H - C - C - C - C - OH
      |   |   |   |
      H   H   H   H
```

22. Wood alcohol is ______________.

(A) $CH_3OH$

(B) $C_3H_7OH$

(C) $C_2H_5OH$

(D) $CH_3COCH_3$

23. The hetero atoms present in ______________.

$CH_3 - CH_2 - O - CH_2 - CH_2Cl$ are

(i) Oxygen

(ii) Chlorine

(iii) Carbon

(iv) Hydrogen

(A) (i) and (ii)      (B) (i) and (iii)

(C) (ii) and (iv)      (D) (i) and (iv)

24. In the soap micelles ______________.

(A) The ionic end of soap is on the surface of the cluster while the carbon chain is in the interior of the cluster.

(B) The ionic end of soap is in the interior of the cluster.

(C) Both ionic end and carbon chain are the exterior of the cluster.

(D) Both ionic end and carbon chain are in the interior of the cluster.

25. Ethanol reacts with sodium and forms two products. These are ______________.

(A) Sodium ethoxide and oxygen

(B) Sodium ethoxide and hydrogen

(C) Sodium ethanoate and oxygen

(D) Sodium ethanoate and hydrogen

26. A covalent bond is formed by ______________.

(A) One sided sharing of electrons

(B) Mutual sharing of electrons

(C) Complete transfer of electrons

(D) Any of the three above

27. Carbon exists in the atmosphere in the form of ______________.

(A) Carbon monoxide

(B) Carbon dioxide

(C) Carbon monoxide in traces and carbon dioxide

(D) Coal

28. Characteristics are given in the following statements which of these statements are correct for carbon compounds?

   (i)   Are good conductors of electricity

   (ii)  Are poor conductors of electricity

   (iii) Have strong forces of attraction between their molecules

   (iv) Do not have strong force of attraction between their molecules

   (A) (i) and (ii)

   (B) (iii) and (iv)

   (C) (ii) and (iv)

   (D) (i) and (iv)

29. The general formula for alkyne is ____________.

   (A) $C_nH_{2n+1}$

   (B) $C_nH_{2n-2}$

   (C) $C_nH_{2n}$

   (D) $C_nH_{2n+2}$

30. Carbon forms a large member of organic compounds due to ____________.

   (A) Catenation

   (B) Tendency to form multiple bonds

   (C) Phenomenon of isomerism

   (D) All of these

## HOTS (ACHIEVERS SECTION)

31. Which of the following is not a saturated hydrocarbon?

   (A) Cyclohexane

   (B) Benzene

   (C) Butane

   (D) Isobutane

32. Carbon forms a large number of organic compounds due to ____________.

   (A) catenation

   (B) phenomenon of isomerism

   (C) tendency to form multiple bonds

   (D) all of these

33. The image represents the structure of a few hydrocarbon compounds.

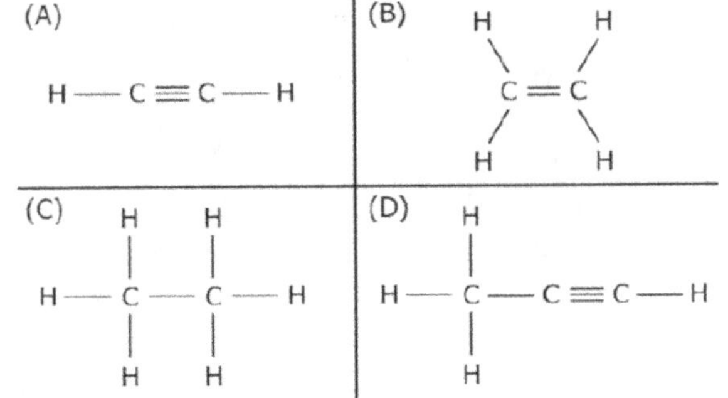

Which of these compounds can be classified as alkynes?

   (A) Only (A)

   (B) Only (B)

   (C) Both (A) and (D)

   (D) Both (B) and (C)

34. The given image represents the structure of a carbon compound known as ethane.

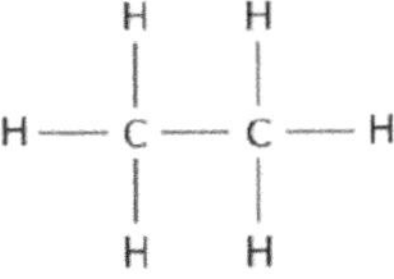

Which of the following option explains the naming of ethane?

   (A) The presence of a functional group connected with a single bond.

   (B) As it contains two carbon atoms, and a single bond connects the carbon atoms.

   (C) Carbon compound with a total number of eight atoms is named ethane.

   (D) As it contains six hydrogen atoms, and a single bond connects the carbon and hydrogen atom.

35. The following chemical reaction shows the addition of chlorine gas to hydrocarbon in the presence of sunlight.

$$CHCl_3 + Cl_2 \rightarrow CCl_4 + HCl$$

How does chlorine react to a hydrocarbon compound in the presence of sunlight?

(A) It adds hydrogen to the compound.

(B) It adds an oxygen atom to the compound.

(C) It substitutes hydrogen atom from the compound.

(D) It breaks double and triple bonds into a single bond.

---

# PERIODIC CLASSIFICATION OF ELEMENTS

## LEARNING OBJECTIVES

➤ Mendeleev's periodic law
➤ Mendeleev's periodic table modern periodic table
➤ Merits, demerits, trends and anomalies of elements

## MULTIPLE CHOICE QUESTIONS

1. Atomic number of the element which is surrounded by elements with atomic numbers 17, 34, 36 and 53 in the modern periodic table is ——————.
   (A) 18       (B) 35
   (C) 37       (D) 52

2. Which of the given element A, B, C, D and E with atomic numbers 2, 3, 7, 10 and 30, respectively belong to the same period?
   (A) A, B, C       (B) B, C, D
   (C) A, D, E       (D) B, D, E

3. The elements A, B, C, D and E have atomic number 9, 11, 17, 12 and 13 respectively. Which pair of elements belong to the same group?
   (A) A and C       (B) A and D
   (C) A and E       (D) B and D

4. Which among the following is the most reactive halogen?
   (A) F       (B) Cl
   (C) Br       (D) I

5. The oxide of which of the following elements is not acidic?
   (A) Cl       (B) S
   (C) Br       (D) Li

6. The correct sequences of atomic radii is ——————.
   (A) Na > Mg > Al > Si
   (B) Si > Al > Mg > Na
   (C) Al > Si > Na > Mg
   (D) Si > Al > Na > Mg

7. Match the items given in column A and column B.

| Column A | Column B |
| --- | --- |
| (i) Uranium | A. Group 17 |
| (ii) Silver | B. Oxygen family |
| (iii) Aluminium | C. Transition element |
| (iv) Fluorine | D. Boron family |
| (v) Sulphur | E. Actinoid |

   (A) (i) – B (ii) – C (iii) – D (iv) – A (v) – E
   (B) (i) – E (ii) – C (iii) – D (iv) – A (v) – B
   (C) (i) – C (ii) – D (iii) – E (iv) – B (v) – A
   (D) (i) – D (ii) – A (iii) – B (iv) – C (v) – D

8. Which of the following statements about the modern period table is correct?
   (A) It has 18 horizontal rows known as periods
   (B) It has 7 vertical columns known as periods

(C) It has 18 vertical columns known as periods

(D) It has 7 horizontal rows known as periods

9. Where would you locate the element with electronic configuration 2, 8 in the modern period table?
   (A) Group 2          (B) Group 8
   (C) Group 10         (D) Group 18

10. Which one of the following elements exhibit maximum number of valence electrons?
    (A) Na              (B) P
    (C) Al              (D) Si

11. Which of the following statements is not correct regarding the trends when going from left to right across the periods of periodic table?
    (A) The number of valence electrons increases
    (B) The atoms lose their electrons more easily
    (C) The elements become less metallic in nature
    (D) The oxides become more acidic

12. An element which is an essential constituent of all organic compounds belongs to ________.
    (A) Group 1         (B) Group 2
    (C) Group 14        (D) Group 15

13. Which of the following gives the correct increasing order of the atomic radii of O, F and N?
    (A) F, O, N         (B) O, F, N
    (C) N, F, O         (D) O, N, F

14. Which of the following elements would lose an electron easily?
    (A) Na              (B) Mg
    (C) Ca              (D) K

15. Which of the following elements does not lose an electron easily?
    (A) Na              (B) Mg
    (C) Al              (D) F

16. Which of the following are the characteristics of isotopes of an element?
    (i) Isotopes of an element have same atomic masses
    (ii) Isotopes of an element have same atomic number
    (iii) Isotopes of an element show same chemical properties
    (iv) Isotopes of an element show same physical properties
    (A) (i) and (iv)        (B) (ii), (iii) and (iv)
    (C) (ii) and (iii)      (D) (ii) and (iv)

17. What type of oxide would Eka-aluminium form?
    (A) $EO_3$              (B) $E_2O_3$
    (C) $E_3O_2$            (D) $EO$

18. Three elements B, Si and Ge are ____________.
    (A) metals
    (B) non-metals
    (C) metalloids
    (D) metal, non-metal and metalloid, respectively

19. Arrange the following elements in the order of the their increasing non-metallic character:
    Li, O, C, Be, F
    (A) F < O < C < Be < Li
    (B) F < C < O < Be < Li
    (C) Li < Be < C < O < F
    (D) F < O < Be < C < Li

20. Which one of the following depicts the correct representation of atomic radius (r) of an atom?

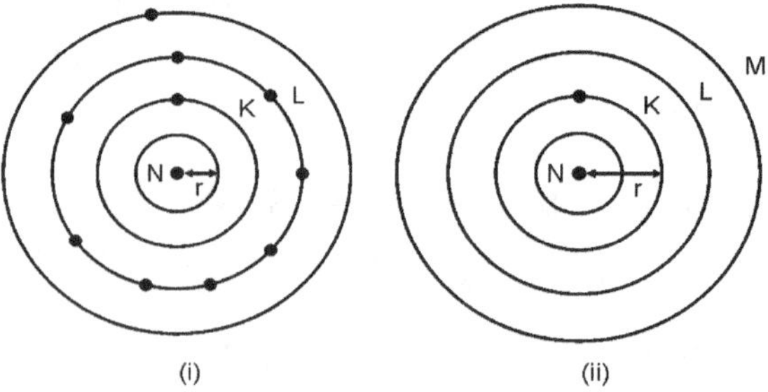

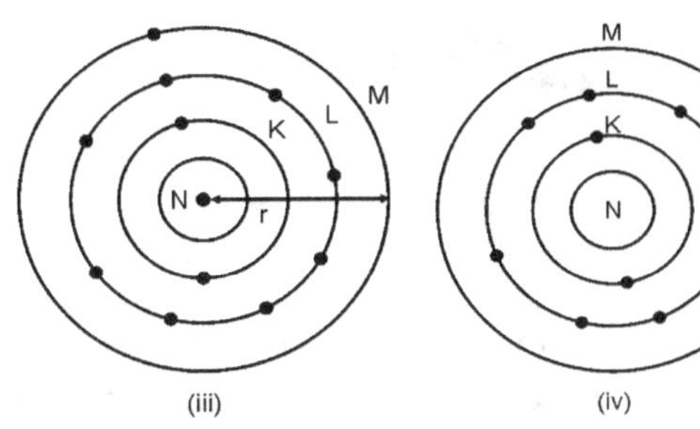

(iii)         (iv)

(A) (i) and (ii)      (B) (i) and (iv)

(C) (ii) and (iii)    (D) (iii) and (iv)

21. Which of the following elements will form an acidic oxide?

   (A) An element with atomic number 3

   (B) An element with atomic number 7

   (C) An element with atomic number 12

   (D) A element with atomic number 19

22. Which of the following set of elements is written in order of their increasing metallic character?

   (A) Na, Li, K

   (B) Be, Mg, Ca

   (C) C, O N

   (D) Mg, Al, Si

23. Match the columns A and B.

| Column A | Column B |
| --- | --- |
| (i) Sulphur | (A) Amphoteric |
| (ii) Fluorine | (B) Radioactive |
| (iii) Aluminium | (C) Yellow solid |
| (iv) Silver | (D) Gas |
| (v) Uranium | (E) Coinage metal |

   (A) (i) – B (ii) – A (iii) – D (iv) – E (v) – C

   (B) (i) – D (ii) – C (iii) – B (iv) – A (v) – E

   (C) (i) – C (ii) – D (iii) – A (iv) – E (v) – B

   (D) (i) – E (ii) – E (iii) – D (iv) – B (v) – A

24. Which of the following does not increase while moving down the group of the periodic table?

   (A) Atomic radius

   (B) Valency

   (C) Metallic character

   (D) Number of shells in an element

25. The element with atomic number 14 is hard and forms acidic oxide and a covalent halide. To which of the following categories does the element belong?

   (A) Metal

   (B) Non-metal

   (C) Metalloid

   (D) Left hand side element

26. The atomic masses of first and the third element of a Dobereiner's triad are 35.5 and 127. What is expected atomic mass of the middle element?

   (A) 23        (B) 40

   (C) 80        (D) 137

27. In which year Mendeleev formulated the law of classification?

   (A) 1865      (B) 1870

   (C) 1869      (D) 1875

28. Who gave modern periodic law?

   (A) Newland      (B) Mendeleev's

   (C) Moseley      (D) Luther Mayer

29. Which group elements are known as alkali metals?

   (A) 1        (B) 2

   (C) 3        (D) 4

30. Who gave the Law of Octaves?

   (A) Moseley      (B) Newland

   (C) Luther Mayer      (D) Mendeleev's

31. Atomic number of the element which is surrounded by elements with atomic numbers 17, 34, 36 and 53 in the modern periodic table is __________.
    (A) 18
    (B) 52
    (C) 37
    (D) 35

32. Which among the following elements has the largest atomic radii?
    (A) Na
    (B) Mg
    (C) K
    (D) Ca

33. A student learns that the atomic size depends on the atomic radius of the elements. How does the atomic radius of elements in the third-period change as one goes from sodium to argon?
    (A) Atomic radius increases from sodium to argon
    (B) Atomic radius decreases from sodium to argon
    (C) Atomic radius increases as new shells are added
    (D) Atomic radius decreases due to the addition of new shells

34. Electronegativity is defined as the ability of an element to form bonds by gaining electrons. How does the electronegativity of elements vary across the periods?
    (A) It increases as the number of shells increases
    (B) It decreases as the number of shells decreases
    (C) It increases as more electrons are added to the same shell
    (D) It decreases as more electrons are added to the same shell.

35. An element X has the atomic number 9. In which period and group can it be placed in the modern periodic table?

(A)

| Period | Group |
| --- | --- |
| 2 | 17 |

(B)

| Period | Group |
| --- | --- |
| 2 | 7 |

(C)

| Period | Group |
| --- | --- |
| 7 | 17 |

(D)

| Period | Group |
| --- | --- |
| 7 | 7 |

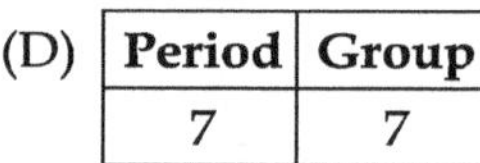

---

Darken Your Choice with HB Pencil

| 1. | Ⓐ Ⓑ Ⓒ Ⓓ | 8. | Ⓐ Ⓑ Ⓒ Ⓓ | 15. | Ⓐ Ⓑ Ⓒ Ⓓ | 22 | Ⓐ Ⓑ Ⓒ Ⓓ | 29. | Ⓐ Ⓑ Ⓒ Ⓓ |
| 2. | Ⓐ Ⓑ Ⓒ Ⓓ | 9. | Ⓐ Ⓑ Ⓒ Ⓓ | 16. | Ⓐ Ⓑ Ⓒ Ⓓ | 23. | Ⓐ Ⓑ Ⓒ Ⓓ | 30. | Ⓐ Ⓑ Ⓒ Ⓓ |
| 3. | Ⓐ Ⓑ Ⓒ Ⓓ | 10. | Ⓐ Ⓑ Ⓒ Ⓓ | 17. | Ⓐ Ⓑ Ⓒ Ⓓ | 24. | Ⓐ Ⓑ Ⓒ Ⓓ | 31. | Ⓐ Ⓑ Ⓒ Ⓓ |
| 4. | Ⓐ Ⓑ Ⓒ Ⓓ | 11. | Ⓐ Ⓑ Ⓒ Ⓓ | 18. | Ⓐ Ⓑ Ⓒ Ⓓ | 25. | Ⓐ Ⓑ Ⓒ Ⓓ | 32. | Ⓐ Ⓑ Ⓒ Ⓓ |
| 5. | Ⓐ Ⓑ Ⓒ Ⓓ | 12. | Ⓐ Ⓑ Ⓒ Ⓓ | 19. | Ⓐ Ⓑ Ⓒ Ⓓ | 26. | Ⓐ Ⓑ Ⓒ Ⓓ | 33. | Ⓐ Ⓑ Ⓒ Ⓓ |
| 6. | Ⓐ Ⓑ Ⓒ Ⓓ | 13. | Ⓐ Ⓑ Ⓒ Ⓓ | 20. | Ⓐ Ⓑ Ⓒ Ⓓ | 27. | Ⓐ Ⓑ Ⓒ Ⓓ | 34. | Ⓐ Ⓑ Ⓒ Ⓓ |
| 7. | Ⓐ Ⓑ Ⓒ Ⓓ | 14. | Ⓐ Ⓑ Ⓒ Ⓓ | 21. | Ⓐ Ⓑ Ⓒ Ⓓ | 28. | Ⓐ Ⓑ Ⓒ Ⓓ | 35. | Ⓐ Ⓑ Ⓒ Ⓓ |

# LIFE PROCESS

## LEARNING OBJECTIVES

➤ Living and non-living
➤ All life processes
➤ Autotrophic and heterotrophic mode of nutrition

## MULTIPLE CHOICE QUESTIONS

1. The two organisms which breathe only through their moist skin are __________.
   - (A) Fish and frog
   - (B) Leech and earthworm
   - (C) Frog and earthworm
   - (D) Fish and earthworm

2. The photosynthesis in a plant is not taking place during the day time if the plant is releasing __________.
   - (A) Water vapour
   - (B) Carbon dioxide
   - (C) Oxygen
   - (D) All of these

3. The breathing and respiration in woody stem of a plant takes place through __________.
   - (A) Lenticels
   - (B) Root hairs
   - (C) Closed stomata
   - (D) Open stomata

4. The end product of glycolysis is __________.
   - (A) Pyruvate
   - (B) ATP
   - (C) ADP
   - (D) Lactic acid

5. During marathon, we sometimes get painful contractions of leg muscles due to the accumulation of one of the following in leg muscles. This is __________.
   - (A) Alcohol
   - (B) Lactose
   - (C) Lactic acid
   - (D) Carbon dioxide

6. In cockroaches, air enters the body through __________.
   - (A) Lungs
   - (B) Gills
   - (C) Skin
   - (D) Spiracles

7. The breakdown of pyruvate to give carbon dioxide, water and energy takes place in __________.
   - (A) Chloroplast
   - (B) Nucleus
   - (C) Cytoplasm
   - (D) Mitochondria

8. Which type of respiration takes place in mitochondria?
   - (A) Aerobic
   - (B) Anaerobic
   - (C) Reduction
   - (D) All of these

9. One of the following does not have a nucleus. This one is _____________.
   (A) Red blood cell
   (B) White blood cell
   (C) Guard cell
   (D) Epidermal cell

10. The lungs are covered in two thin membranes called _____________.
   (A) Alveoli            (B) Thoracic cavity
   (C) Ventilator         (D) Pleura

11. Ultrafiltration occurs in _____________.
   (A) Henle's loop
   (B) Proximal convoluted tubule
   (C) Distal convoluted tubule
   (D) Bowman's capsule

12. Match the column A to column B.

| Column A | Column B |
|---|---|
| (A) Aerobic respiration | 1. Trachea |
| (B) Cartilaginous rings | 2. Xylem |
| (C) Transport of hormones | 3. Presence of oxygen |
| (D) Ascent of rap | 4. Blood |

|     | A | B | C | D |
|-----|---|---|---|---|
| (A) | 1 | 2 | 3 | 4 |
| (B) | 3 | 1 | 4 | 2 |
| (C) | 3 | 2 | 1 | 4 |
| (D) | 2 | 4 | 3 | 2 |

13. One of the following is not a constituent of blood. This one is _____________.
   (A) Platelets
   (B) Sieve plates
   (C) Red blood cells
   (D) White blood cells

14. Which vein brings clean blood from the lungs into the heart?
   (A) Renal vein
   (B) Hepatic vein
   (C) Pulmonary vein
   (D) Vena cava

15. Which blood vessel does not carry any carbon dioxide?
   (A) Pulmonary artery
   (B) Pulmonary vein
   (C) Vena cava
   (D) Hepatic vein

16. If a patient is put on dialysis, he is most likely suffering from a severe aliment of the _____________.
   (A) Circulatory system
   (B) Excretory system
   (C) Digestive system
   (D) Respiratory system

17. Which one of the following has cytoplasm but no nucleus _____________.
   (A) Xylem vessel        (B) Tracheid
   (C) Companion           (D) Sieve tube

18. The process of carrying food from the leaves to other parts of a plant is called _____________.
   (A) Transportation
   (B) Translocation
   (C) Transpiration
   (D) Transformation

19. Which of the following is the only conducting tissue in non-flowering plants?
   (A) Sieve tubes
   (B) Tracheids
   (C) Xylem vessels
   (D) Companion cells

20. Which one of following does not have valves?
   (A) Heart               (B) Veins
   (C) Arteries            (D) Capillaries

21. Coagulation of blood in a cut or wound is brought about by _____________.
   (A) RBC                 (B) WBC
   (C) Platelets           (D) Plasma

22. The instrument for measuring blood pressure is called _____________.
    (A) Manometer
    (B) Barometer
    (C) Potentiometer
    (D) Sphygmomanometer

23. The excretory unit in the human excretory system is called _____________.
    (A) Neuron          (B) Nephron
    (C) Nephridia       (D) Kidneyon

24. What prevents the backflow of blood inside the heart during contraction?
    (A) Thin wall of atria
    (B) Thick muscular walls of ventricles
    (C) Valves
    (D) All of these

25. Which of the following is the correct path taken by urine in our body?
    (A) Kidney → water → urethra → bladder
    (B) Kidney → ureter → bladder → urethra
    (C) Kidney → bladder → urethra → ureter
    (D) Bladder → kidney → ureter → urethra

26. The substance which is not reabsorbed into the blood capillaries surrounding the tubule of a nephron is mainly _____________.
    (A) Glucose         (B) Urea
    (C) Water           (D) Amino acid

27. The wave of expansion of an artery when blood is forced into it is called _____________.
    (A) Heart beat
    (B) Pulse
    (C) Flow
    (D) Ticking

28. An animal having double circulation in three-chambered heart is _____________.
    (A) Snake           (B) Deer
    (C) Sparrow         (D) Fish

29. Which of the following statements are correct?
    (i)   Pyruvate can be converted into ethanol and carbon dioxide by yeast
    (ii)  Fermentation takes place in the case of aerobic bacteria
    (iii) Fermentation takes place in mitochondria
    (iv)  Fermentation is a form of anaerobic respiration
    (A) (i) and (iii)
    (B) (i) and (iv)
    (C) (ii) and (iv)
    (D) (ii) and (iii)

30. The opening and closing of stomatal pores depends upon _____________.
    (A) Oxygen
    (B) Temperature
    (C) Water in guard cells
    (D) Concentration of $CO_2$ in stomata

## HOTS (ACHIEVERS SECTION)

31. During respiration, the exchange of gases takes places in _____________.
    (A) Bronchi         (B) Alveoli
    (C) Bronchioles     (D) Trachea

32. Human respiratory pigment is:
    (A) Insulin         (B) Haemoglobin
    (C) Thyrocin        (D) Melanin

33. The phloem tissue in plants is responsible for the transport of _____________.
    (A) Water
    (B) Sugar
    (C) Water and minerals
    (D) All of these

34. A big tree falls in a forest but its roots are still in contact with the soil. The branches of this fallen tree grow straight up. This happens in response to ——————.
(A) Water and light
(B) Water and air
(C) Light and gravity
(D) Gravity and air

35. Which of the following acts as a stimulus in the process of hydrotropism?
(A) Hydrocarbon
(B) Hydrogen oxide
(C) Hydrogen chloride
(D) Hydrogen peroxide

| 1. | Ⓐ Ⓑ Ⓒ Ⓓ | 8. | Ⓐ Ⓑ Ⓒ Ⓓ | 15. | Ⓐ Ⓑ Ⓒ Ⓓ | 22 | Ⓐ Ⓑ Ⓒ Ⓓ | 29. | Ⓐ Ⓑ Ⓒ Ⓓ |
| 2. | Ⓐ Ⓑ Ⓒ Ⓓ | 9. | Ⓐ Ⓑ Ⓒ Ⓓ | 16. | Ⓐ Ⓑ Ⓒ Ⓓ | 23. | Ⓐ Ⓑ Ⓒ Ⓓ | 30. | Ⓐ Ⓑ Ⓒ Ⓓ |
| 3. | Ⓐ Ⓑ Ⓒ Ⓓ | 10. | Ⓐ Ⓑ Ⓒ Ⓓ | 17. | Ⓐ Ⓑ Ⓒ Ⓓ | 24. | Ⓐ Ⓑ Ⓒ Ⓓ | 31. | Ⓐ Ⓑ Ⓒ Ⓓ |
| 4. | Ⓐ Ⓑ Ⓒ Ⓓ | 11. | Ⓐ Ⓑ Ⓒ Ⓓ | 18. | Ⓐ Ⓑ Ⓒ Ⓓ | 25. | Ⓐ Ⓑ Ⓒ Ⓓ | 32. | Ⓐ Ⓑ Ⓒ Ⓓ |
| 5. | Ⓐ Ⓑ Ⓒ Ⓓ | 12. | Ⓐ Ⓑ Ⓒ Ⓓ | 19. | Ⓐ Ⓑ Ⓒ Ⓓ | 26. | Ⓐ Ⓑ Ⓒ Ⓓ | 33. | Ⓐ Ⓑ Ⓒ Ⓓ |
| 6. | Ⓐ Ⓑ Ⓒ Ⓓ | 13. | Ⓐ Ⓑ Ⓒ Ⓓ | 20. | Ⓐ Ⓑ Ⓒ Ⓓ | 27. | Ⓐ Ⓑ Ⓒ Ⓓ | 34. | Ⓐ Ⓑ Ⓒ Ⓓ |
| 7. | Ⓐ Ⓑ Ⓒ Ⓓ | 14. | Ⓐ Ⓑ Ⓒ Ⓓ | 21. | Ⓐ Ⓑ Ⓒ Ⓓ | 28. | Ⓐ Ⓑ Ⓒ Ⓓ | 35. | Ⓐ Ⓑ Ⓒ Ⓓ |

# REPRODUCTION IN ORGANISM

## LEARNING OBJECTIVES

➤ The importance of variation
➤ Various methods of asexual reproduction
➤ Sexual reproduction in flowering plants

## MULTIPLE CHOICE QUESTIONS

1. AIDS is a deadly disease which is caused by ____________.
   - (A) A protozoan
   - (B) A virus
   - (C) A fungus
   - (D) A bacterium

2. Which one of the following best describes the function of the umbilical cord? It ____________.
   - (A) Supplies oxygenated blood from the mother to the embryo
   - (B) Feeds of the embryo with digested substances
   - (C) Carries nutrients and wastes to and from the embryo
   - (D) Removes waste from the embryo to the mother's blood

3. The normal body cell of an organism contains 28 pairs of chromosomes. The number of chromosomes present in its germ cell will be ____________.
   - (A) 14
   - (B) 42
   - (C) 28
   - (D) 56

4. The male gametes in a flower and in a human are produced respectively in ____________.
   - (A) Stigma and ovary
   - (B) Ovary and testes
   - (C) Anther and testes
   - (D) Anther and style

5. Which of the following flowers is bisexual?
   - (A) Jasmine
   - (B) Hibiscus
   - (C) Lotus
   - (D) Rose

6. The disease kala-azar is caused by a microorganism is known as ____________.
   - (A) Leech
   - (B) Leishmania
   - (C) Planaria
   - (D) Plasmodium

7. Which of the following animal shows external fertilisation?
   - (A) Goat
   - (B) Reptiles
   - (C) Toads
   - (D) Birds

8. The protozoan having a flagellum at its one end is ____________.
   - (A) Hydra
   - (B) Leishmania
   - (C) Paramecium
   - (D) Amoeba

9. A simple multicellular animal having tentacles which lives in fresh water usually reproduces by the asexual process of ____________.
   - (A) Spore formation
   - (B) Fragmentation
   - (C) Budding
   - (D) Binary fission

10. Binary fission describes the type of reproduction where the organism divides to form ____________.
    (A) Many buds
    (B) Two daughters
    (C) Two hyphal
    (D) Many spores

11. Vegetative propagation refers to the formation of new plants from which of the following existing organs of the old plants?
    (A) Stems, roots and flowers
    (B) Stems, leaves and flowers
    (C) Stems, roots and leaves
    (D) Stem, flowers and fruits

12. Which one of the following is a male sex chromosome?
    (A) XX
    (B) YY
    (C) XY
    (D) All of these

13. The sexually transmitted disease which is caused by bacteria is ____________.
    (A) Malaria
    (B) Gonorrhoea
    (C) AIDS
    (D) Diarrhoea

14. In which one of the following birth control methods, a small portion of oviducts of a woman is removed by surgical operation and the cut ends are ligated?
    (A) Copper-T
    (B) Vasectomy
    (C) Tubectomy
    (D) Diaphragm

15. The ratio of number of chromosomes in a human zygote and a human sperm is ____________.
    (A) 2 : 1
    (B) 3 : 1
    (C) 1 : 2
    (D) 1 : 3

16. The advantage of internal fertilisation over external fertilisation is that in internal fertilisation ____________.
    (A) Copulation and fusion of gametes is passive
    (B) Fewer individuals are produced
    (C) New off-springs are exactly like the parent
    (D) Production of large numbers of gametes is unnecessary

17. In a flower, the parts that produce male and female gametes are ________ respectively:
    (A) Filament and stigma
    (B) Anther and ovary
    (C) Stamen and style
    (D) Sepal and anther

18. Characters that are transmitted from parents to offspring during sexual reproduction show ____________.
    (A) Only similarities with parents
    (B) Only variations with parents
    (C) Both similarities and variations with parents
    (D) Neither similarities nor variations with parents

19. The length of pollen tube depends on the distance between ____________.
    (A) Upper surface of stigma and lower part of style
    (B) Pollen grain and upper surface of stigma
    (C) Pollen grain on upper surface of stigma and ovule
    (D) Pollen grain in anther and upper surface of stigma

20. In human males, the testes lie in the scrotum outside the body because it helps in the ____________.
    (A) Process of mating
    (B) Easy transfer of sperms
    (C) Formation of sperms
    (D) All of these

21. Which of the following statements are true for flowers?
    (i) Flowers are always bisexual
    (ii) They contain sexual reproductive organs

(iii) They are produce in all groups of plants

(iv) After fertilisation they give rise to fruits

(A) (i) and (ii)  
(B) (ii) and (iii)  
(C) (ii) and (iv)  
(D) (i) and (iv)

22. The correct sequence of organs in the male reproductive system for the transport of sperm is ——————.

(A) Testes → vas deferens → ureter  
(B) Testes → vas deferens → urethra  
(C) Testes → ureter → urethra  
(D) Testes → urethra → ureter

23. In the figure given alongside, the parts A, B and C marked sequentially are ——————.

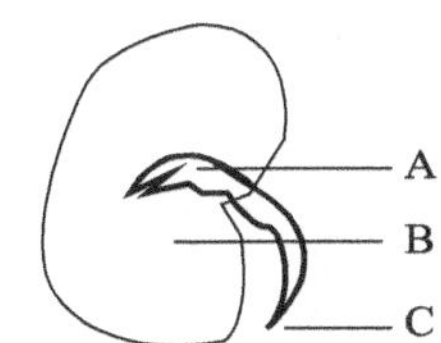


(A) Plumule, radical and cotyledon  
(B) Radical, cotyledon and plumule  
(C) Plumule, cotyledon and radical  
(D) Cotyledon, plumule and radical

24. One of the following processes does not lead to the formation of clones. This is ——————.

(A) Fragmentation  
(B) Fission  
(C) Fertilisation  
(D) Tissue culture

25. In human females, an event that indicates the onset of reproductive phase is ——————.

(A) Growth of body  
(B) Change in voice  
(C) Menstruation  
(D) Change in hair pattern

26. The number of chromosomes in parents and offsprings of a particular species remains constant due to ——————.

(A) Doubling of chromosomes after gamete formation  
(B) Halving of chromosomes after gamete formation  
(C) Doubling of chromosomes after zygote formation  
(D) Halving of chromosomes during gamete formation

27. The figure given alongside show the human male reproductive organs, which structures make sperms and seminal fluid?

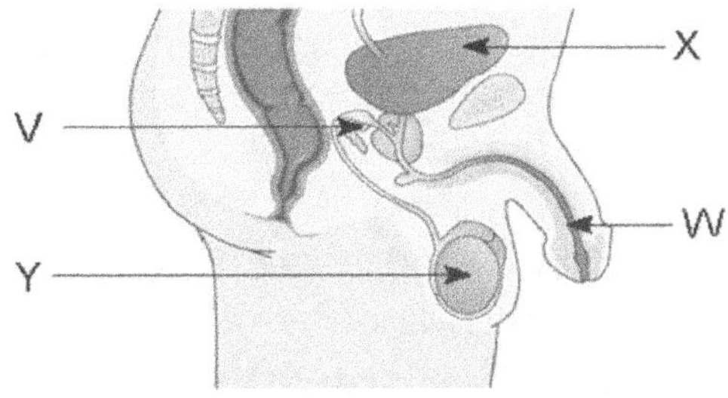


(A) X makes sperms and W makes seminal fluid  
(B) Y makes sperms and V makes seminal fluid  
(C) V makes sperms and X makes seminal fluid  
(D) W makes sperms and Y makes seminal fluid

28. Match the organisms given in column I with the methods of reproduction/propagation given in column II.

| Column I | Column II |
| --- | --- |
| (i) Potatoes | A. Spore formation |
| (ii) Rhizopus | B. Binary fission |
| (iii) Hydra | C. Tubers |
| (iv) Planaria | D. Budding |
| (v) Leishmania | E. Regeneration |

(A) (i) → B (ii) → C (iii) → E (iv) → A (v) → D  
(B) (i) → C (ii) → A (iii) → D (iv) → E (v) → B  
(C) (i) → D (ii) → E (iii) → B (iv) → C (v) → A  
(D) (i) → E (ii) → D (iii) → A (iv) → B (v) → C

29. In spirogyra asexual reproduction takes place by ______________.
   (A) Division of a cell into two cells
   (B) Division of a cell into many cells
   (C) Breaking up of filaments into smaller bits
   (D) Formation of a large number of buds

30. An organism having a whip-like structure of one end which reproduces by the process of binary fission is ______________.
   (A) Hydra
   (B) Leishmania
   (C) Plasmodium
   (D) Paramecium

## HOTS (ACHIEVERS SECTION)

31. The ability of a cell to divide into several cells during reproduction in plasmodium is called ______________.
   (A) budding
   (B) fragmentation
   (C) binary fission
   (D) multiple fission

32. In order to give birth to a baby girl:
   (A) Y gamete fertilizes X egg
   (B) X gamete fertilizes X egg
   (C) Y gamete fertilizes Y egg
   (D) None of these

33. A trait in an organism is influenced by ______________.
   (A) Paternal DNA only
   (B) Maternal DNA only
   (C) Both maternal and paternal DNA
   (D) Neither by paternal nor by maternal DNA

34. The number of pair(s) of sex chromosomes in the zygote of human is ______________.
   (A) One                     (B) Two
   (C) Three                   (D) Four

35. A plant with two small genes breed with a plant with two tall genes to produce ______________.
   (A) All small plants
   (B) All tall plants
   (C) Small plants and tall plants in the ratio 1 : 3
   (D) Tall plants and small plants in the ratio 3 : 1

---



| 1. | Ⓐ Ⓑ Ⓒ Ⓓ | 8. | Ⓐ Ⓑ Ⓒ Ⓓ | 15. | Ⓐ Ⓑ Ⓒ Ⓓ | 22 | Ⓐ Ⓑ Ⓒ Ⓓ | 29. | Ⓐ Ⓑ Ⓒ Ⓓ |
| 2. | Ⓐ Ⓑ Ⓒ Ⓓ | 9. | Ⓐ Ⓑ Ⓒ Ⓓ | 16. | Ⓐ Ⓑ Ⓒ Ⓓ | 23. | Ⓐ Ⓑ Ⓒ Ⓓ | 30. | Ⓐ Ⓑ Ⓒ Ⓓ |
| 3. | Ⓐ Ⓑ Ⓒ Ⓓ | 10. | Ⓐ Ⓑ Ⓒ Ⓓ | 17. | Ⓐ Ⓑ Ⓒ Ⓓ | 24. | Ⓐ Ⓑ Ⓒ Ⓓ | 31. | Ⓐ Ⓑ Ⓒ Ⓓ |
| 4. | Ⓐ Ⓑ Ⓒ Ⓓ | 11. | Ⓐ Ⓑ Ⓒ Ⓓ | 18. | Ⓐ Ⓑ Ⓒ Ⓓ | 25. | Ⓐ Ⓑ Ⓒ Ⓓ | 32. | Ⓐ Ⓑ Ⓒ Ⓓ |
| 5. | Ⓐ Ⓑ Ⓒ Ⓓ | 12. | Ⓐ Ⓑ Ⓒ Ⓓ | 19. | Ⓐ Ⓑ Ⓒ Ⓓ | 26. | Ⓐ Ⓑ Ⓒ Ⓓ | 33. | Ⓐ Ⓑ Ⓒ Ⓓ |
| 6. | Ⓐ Ⓑ Ⓒ Ⓓ | 13. | Ⓐ Ⓑ Ⓒ Ⓓ | 20. | Ⓐ Ⓑ Ⓒ Ⓓ | 27. | Ⓐ Ⓑ Ⓒ Ⓓ | 34. | Ⓐ Ⓑ Ⓒ Ⓓ |
| 7. | Ⓐ Ⓑ Ⓒ Ⓓ | 14. | Ⓐ Ⓑ Ⓒ Ⓓ | 21. | Ⓐ Ⓑ Ⓒ Ⓓ | 28. | Ⓐ Ⓑ Ⓒ Ⓓ | 35. | Ⓐ Ⓑ Ⓒ Ⓓ |

# HEREDITY AND EVOLUTION

## MULTIPLE CHOICE QUESTIONS

1. Beside human beings, XX-XY sex determination mechanism is depicted by __________.
   - (A) A snake
   - (B) A turtle
   - (C) A lizard
   - (D) A crocodile

2. Which one of the following is not present in the Darwin's theory of evolution?
   - (A) Over population
   - (B) Natural selection
   - (C) Struggle for existence
   - (D) Use and disuse of organ

3. The presence of which of the following types of organs in two organisms indicates that they are derived from the same ancestor?
   - (A) Homologous organs
   - (B) Analogous organs
   - (C) Digestive organs
   - (D) Respiratory organs

4. The fossil trilobite was originally __________.
   - (A) An ave
   - (B) A reptile
   - (C) An invertebrate
   - (D) An arthropod

5. The presence of which of the following types of organs in two animals indicates that they are not derived from the same ancestor?
   - (A) Homologous organs
   - (B) Analogous organs
   - (C) Excretory organs
   - (D) Reproductive organs

6. One pair of organs in the following animals are not homologous. This is __________.
   - (A) Forelimbs in lizard and frog
   - (B) Forelimbs in human and lizard
   - (C) Wings in butterfly and bat
   - (D) Wings in bat and bird

7. The wings of a housefly and the wings of a sparrow are an example of __________.
   - (A) Homologous organs
   - (B) Analogous organs
   - (C) vestigial organs
   - (D) respiratory organs

8. According to evolutionary theory, the formation of new species is generally due to the __________.
   - (A) Sudden creation by nature
   - (B) Movement of individuals from one habitat to another
   - (C) Accumulation variations over several generations
   - (D) Clones formed during asexual reproduction

9. One of the following traits of the parents cannot be passed on to their future generations. This trait is ____________.
   (A) Pointed chin      (B) Scarred chin
   (C) Broad chin        (D) Cleft chin

10. There are two structures as shown:
    (i) Stem tendril in passiflora and
    (ii) Thorn of Bougainvillea



    These two are ____________.
    (A) Homologous organs
    (B) Analogous organs
    (C) Vestigial organs
    (D) Heterologus organs

11. Archacopteryx was having characters of ____________.
    (A) Invertebrates and vertebrates
    (B) Fishes and amphibians
    (C) Reptiles and birds
    (D) Birds and mammals

12. The visible characteristic in an organism is known as ____________.
    (A) Genotype      (B) Phenotype
    (C) Prototype     (D) Stereotype

13. The following results were obtained by a scientist who crossed the $F_1$ generation of pure-breeding parents for round and wrinkled seeds:

    Dominant trait          Recessive trait

    No. of F2 offspring      Round seeds

    Wrinkled seeds 7524

    From these results, it can be concluded that the actual number of round seeds that obtained was ____________.
    (A) 1881      (B) 2508
    (C) 5643      (D) 22572

14. A trait in an organism is influenced by ____________.
    (A) Material DNA only
    (B) Paternal DNA only
    (C) Both maternal and paternal DNA
    (D) Neither by paternal nor by maternal DNA

15. The exchange of genetic material takes place in ____________.
    (A) Budding
    (B) Sexual reproduction
    (C) Asexual reproduction
    (D) Vegetative reproduction

16. A cross between a tall plant (TT) and short plant (tt) resulted in progeny that were all tall plants because ____________.
    (A) Tallness is dominant trait
    (B) Tallness is recessive trait
    (C) Shortness is the dominant trait
    (D) Height of plant is not governed by gene trait

17. Match the terms given in column I with those given in column II.

| Column I | Column II |
| --- | --- |
| (i) Fossil | (A) A famous evolutionist |
| (ii) A theory of evolution | (B) Survival of the fittest |
| (iii) Probable ancestor of bird | (C) Petrified remains of prehistoric life |
| (iv) Charles Darwin | (D) Father of genetics |
| (v) Gregor Mendel | (E) Archaeopteryx |

    (A) (i) → B, (ii) → C, (iii) → A, (iv) → E, (v) → D
    (B) (i) → C, (ii) → B, (iii) → E, (iv) → A, (v) → D
    (C) (i) → E, (ii) → D, (iii) → B, (iv) → C, (v) → A
    (D) (i) → D, (ii) → A, (iii) → C, (iv) → B, (v) → E

18. One of the following traits cannot be inherited. This one is ____________.
    (A) Colour of eyes      (B) Colour of skin
    (C) Nature of hair      (D) Size of body



OLYMPIAD WORKBOOK (NSO) CLASS– 10

19. Which of the following statements is incorrect with respect to variations?
   (A) Change in genetic composition results in variations
   (B) Selection of variations of environmental factors form the basis of evolutionary process
   (C) All variations in a species have equal chances of survival
   (D) Variations are minimum in asexual reproduction

20. Wings of an insect and forelimbs of a birds are __________.
   (A) Homologous organs
   (B) Analogous organs
   (C) Analeptic organs
   (D) Homophobic organs

21. One of the following has not been produced from wild cabbage by the process of artificial selection. This one is __________.
   (A) Cabbage          (B) Spinach
   (C) Kale             (D) Kohlrabi

22. The organs which perform different functions but have the same basic structure are known as __________.
   (A) Homologous organs
   (B) Analogous organs
   (C) Hemolytic organs
   (D) Analytic organs

23. One of the following characteristics of the parents can be inherited by their children. This is __________.
   (A) Technique of swimming
   (B) Cut nose
   (C) Snub nose
   (D) Deep scar in chin

24. In human males all the chromosomes are paired perfectly except one. This/these unpaired chromosomes is/are __________.
   (i)   Small chromosome
   (ii)  Large chromosome
   (iii) Y chromosome
   (iv)  X chromosome
   (A) (i) and (ii)       (B) (ii) and (iii)
   (C) (iii) and (iv)     (D) (ii) and (iv)

25. The sex of a child is determined by which of the following __________.
   (A) The length of time between volution and copulation
   (B) The presence of a Y chromosome in a sperm
   (C) The presence of an X chromosome in an ovum
   (D) The length of the mother's pregnancy

26. The zygote which has inherited an X chromosome from the father will develop into __________.
   (A) Adult              (B) Baby boy
   (C) Baby girl          (D) Either boy or girl

27. Which of the following statements is incorrect?
   (A) For every hormone there is a gene
   (B) For every type of fat there is a gene
   (C) For every protein there is a gene
   (D) For production of every enzyme there is a gene

28. If the fossil of an organism is found in the deeper layer of earth, then we can predict that __________.
   (A) The extinction of organism has occurred recently
   (B) The fossil position in the layers of earth is not related to its time of extinction
   (C) The extinction of organism has occurred thousands of years ago
   (D) Time of the extinction cannot be determined

29. Some dinosaurs had feathers although they could not fly but birds have feathers that help them to fly. In the context of evolution, this means that __________.
   (A) Feathers are homologous structures in both the organisms
   (B) There is no evolutionary connection between reptiles and birds
   (C) Reptiles have evolved from birds
   (D) Birds have evolved from reptiles

30. New species may be formed if __________.
   (i) There is no change in genetic material
   (ii) Chromosome number change in the gamete
   (iii) DNA undergoes significant changes in germ cells
   (iv) Mating does not take place
   (A) (i) and (ii)    (B) (ii) and (iii)
   (C) (iii) and (iv)    (D) (i) and (iv)

## HOTS (ACHIEVERS SECTION)

31. The transmission of the __________ from one generation to the next is called heredity.
   (A) Trait    (B) Specification
   (C) Variations    (D) Properties

32. The evolution of new organism is also called __________.
   (A) Organic evolution
   (B) Anatomical evolution
   (C) Biochemical evolution
   (D) Behavioral evolution

33. Two pea plants, one with round green seeds (RRyy) and another with wrinkled yellow (rrYY) seeds, produce F1 progeny that have round yellow (RrYy) seeds. When F1 plants are self-pollinated, the F2 progeny will have a new combination of characters. Choose the new combinations from the following:
   (i) Round, yellow
   (ii) Round, green
   (iii) Wrinkled, yellow
   (iv) Wrinkled, green
   (A) (i) and (ii)    (B) (i) and (iv)
   (C) (ii) and (iii)    (D) (i) and (iii)

34. Which of the following statements is not true with respect to variation?
   (A) All variations in a species have equal chances of survival.
   (B) Change in genetic composition results in variation.
   (C) Selection of variants by environmental factors forms the basis of evolutionary processes.
   (D) Variation is minimum in asexual reproduction.

35. In pea plants, yellow seeds are dominant to green seeds. If a heterozygous yellow-seeded plant is crossed with a green-seeded plant, what ratio of yellow and green-seeded plants would you expect in the $F_1$ generation?
   (A) 9:1    (B) 3:1
   (C) 1:3    (D) 50:50

---

Darken Your Choice with HB Pencil

| | A B C D | | A B C D | | A B C D | | A B C D | | A B C D |
|---|---|---|---|---|---|---|---|---|---|---|
| 1. | Ⓐ Ⓑ Ⓒ Ⓓ | 8. | Ⓐ Ⓑ Ⓒ Ⓓ | 15. | Ⓐ Ⓑ Ⓒ Ⓓ | 22 | Ⓐ Ⓑ Ⓒ Ⓓ | 29. | Ⓐ Ⓑ Ⓒ Ⓓ |
| 2. | Ⓐ Ⓑ Ⓒ Ⓓ | 9. | Ⓐ Ⓑ Ⓒ Ⓓ | 16. | Ⓐ Ⓑ Ⓒ Ⓓ | 23. | Ⓐ Ⓑ Ⓒ Ⓓ | 30. | Ⓐ Ⓑ Ⓒ Ⓓ |
| 3. | Ⓐ Ⓑ Ⓒ Ⓓ | 10. | Ⓐ Ⓑ Ⓒ Ⓓ | 17. | Ⓐ Ⓑ Ⓒ Ⓓ | 24. | Ⓐ Ⓑ Ⓒ Ⓓ | 31. | Ⓐ Ⓑ Ⓒ Ⓓ |
| 4. | Ⓐ Ⓑ Ⓒ Ⓓ | 11. | Ⓐ Ⓑ Ⓒ Ⓓ | 18. | Ⓐ Ⓑ Ⓒ Ⓓ | 25. | Ⓐ Ⓑ Ⓒ Ⓓ | 32. | Ⓐ Ⓑ Ⓒ Ⓓ |
| 5. | Ⓐ Ⓑ Ⓒ Ⓓ | 12. | Ⓐ Ⓑ Ⓒ Ⓓ | 19. | Ⓐ Ⓑ Ⓒ Ⓓ | 26. | Ⓐ Ⓑ Ⓒ Ⓓ | 33. | Ⓐ Ⓑ Ⓒ Ⓓ |
| 6. | Ⓐ Ⓑ Ⓒ Ⓓ | 13. | Ⓐ Ⓑ Ⓒ Ⓓ | 20. | Ⓐ Ⓑ Ⓒ Ⓓ | 27. | Ⓐ Ⓑ Ⓒ Ⓓ | 34. | Ⓐ Ⓑ Ⓒ Ⓓ |
| 7. | Ⓐ Ⓑ Ⓒ Ⓓ | 14. | Ⓐ Ⓑ Ⓒ Ⓓ | 21. | Ⓐ Ⓑ Ⓒ Ⓓ | 28. | Ⓐ Ⓑ Ⓒ Ⓓ | 35. | Ⓐ Ⓑ Ⓒ Ⓓ |

# LIGHT

## LEARNING OBJECTIVES

➤ The dual nature of light
➤ Reflection and state its laws
➤ Plane mirror and its characteristics
➤ Concave and convex mirrors as a part of spherical mirror

## MULTIPLE CHOICE QUESTIONS

1. The focal length of a concave mirror that produces four times larger real image of an object held at 5 cm from the mirror is __________.

   (A) −4 cm      (B) −20 cm
   (C) 20 cm      (D) 5 cm

2. When two or more than two rays starting from a point on the object, after refraction through a lens, do not actually meet but appear to diverge from point, the image formed is __________.

   (A) Virtual      (B) Real
   (C) Inverted      (D) None of these

3. A ray of light falling normally on a plane mirror on reflection __________.

   (A) Retraces its path
   (B) Deviate through 90°
   (C) Reflect parallel to the mirror
   (D) Do not reflect at all

4. A concave mirror produces an image of 20 cm height which is five times magnified. The height of the object is __________.

   (A) 10 cm      (B) 2 cm
   (C) 4 cm      (D) 5 cm

5. If an object is placed at a distance of 10 cm in front of a plane mirror, how far would it be from its image __________.

   (A) 10 cm      (B) 20 cm
   (C) 40 cm      (D) 5 cm

6. The linear magnification of a convex mirror of focal length 15 cm is $\frac{1}{3}$. The distance of the object from the mirror is __________.

   (A) +15 cm      (B) −15 cm
   (C) +30 cm      (D) −30 cm

7. If you want to get an image of the object in inverted position at $2F_2$, the object should be placed at __________.

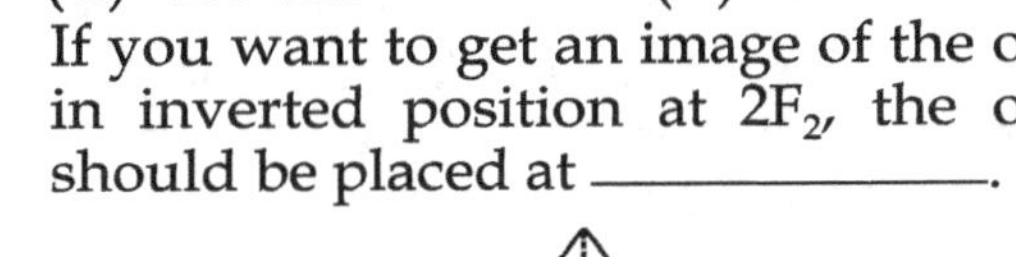
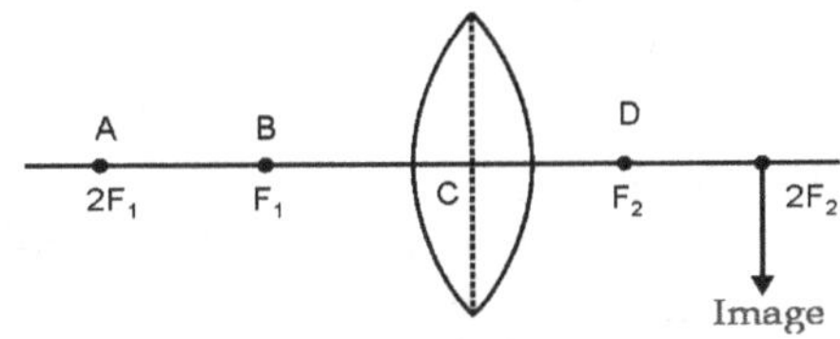



   (A) Between A and C
   (B) Between B and C
   (C) At A
   (D) At B

8. The power of a convex lens $P_1$ is equal to 4 D, which is placed in close contact with a concave lens having power $P_2$ equal to −10 D. What will be the power of the combination of the two lenses?

   (A) −6 D      (B) 6 D
   (C) 40 D      (D) −40 D

**Direction (9 – 11):** See the given below diagram and answer the questions.

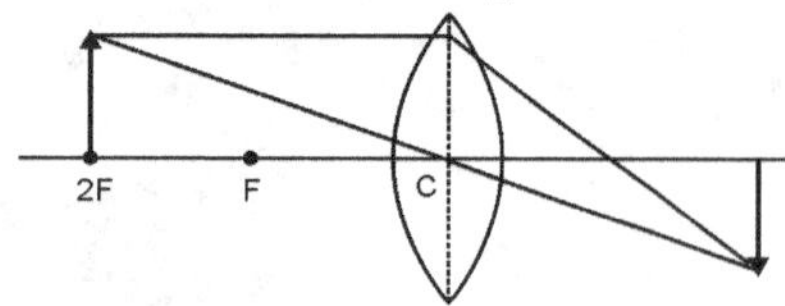

9. If the height of the object is 1 cm, what will be the size of the image if the object is placed at a distance of 2F?
   (A) 2 cm          (B) 4 cm
   (C) 1 cm          (D) 8 cm

10. The above lens is a ____________.
   (A) Concave lens
   (B) Convex lens
   (C) Concave convex lens
   (D) Convex concave lens

11. The ray of light parallel to the principal axis of a convex lens will pass after refraction ____________.
   (A) Through F
   (B) Through 2F
   (C) Between F and 2F
   (D) Between C and F

12. The image of a small electric bulb fixed on the wall of a room is to be obtained, on the opposite wall 3 m away by means of a large convex lens. What is the maximum possible focal length of the lens required for the purpose?
   (A) 0.25 m          (B) 0.50 m
   (C) 1 m            (D) 0.75 m

13. A concave lens is kept in contact with a convex lens of focal length 20 cm. The combination works as converging lens of the focal length 100 cm. The power of concave lens is ____________.
   (A) –D             (B) –2 D
   (C) –4 D           (D) 4 D

14. The linear magnification of a convex lens is –1 when object in front of the lens is ____________.
   (A) At infinity
   (B) At focus
   (C) At $2F_1$
   (D) Between $F_1$ and $2F_1$

15. An object is held at 40 cm from a concave lens of focal length 60 cm. The distance of the image from the lens is ____________.
   (A) –24 cm          (B) 24 cm
   (C) –60 cm          (D) +60 cm

16. If a glass is placed in a liquid of refractive index that is equal to glass, it will ____________.
   (A) Enlarge
   (B) Disappear
   (C) Shine
   (D) Become tiny

17. The focal length of a combination of convex lens of power 1 D and concave lens of power –1.5 D is ____________.
   (A) –0.5 m          (B) –1.5 m
   (C) –2 m            (D) 2.5 m

18. A concave mirror produces three times magnified real image of an object placed at 10 cm in front of it. The image is located at ____________.
   (A) 30 cm in front of the mirror
   (B) 30 cm behind the mirror
   (C) 60 cm in front of the mirror
   (D) 60 cm behind the mirror

19. One dioptre is the power of lens of focal length ____________.
   (A) 100 metre
   (B) 1 metre
   (C) 10 metre
   (D) 1 centimetre

20. The power of a concave lens of focal length 2 m is ____________.
   (A) –0.5 D          (B) 0.5 D
   (C) 2 D            (D) –2 D

21. Which of the following can make a parallel beam of light when light from a point source incident on it?
   (A) Convex mirror as well as concave lens
   (B) Concave mirror as well as convex lens
   (C) Both concave and convex mirror
   (D) Both concave and convex lens



OLYMPIAD WORKBOOK (NSO) CLASS– 10

22. A beam of light is incident through the holes on side A and emerge out of the holes on the side B of the box as shown in the figure? Which of the following could be inside the box?
(A) Concave lens
(B) Rectangular glass slab
(C) Convex lens
(D) Prism

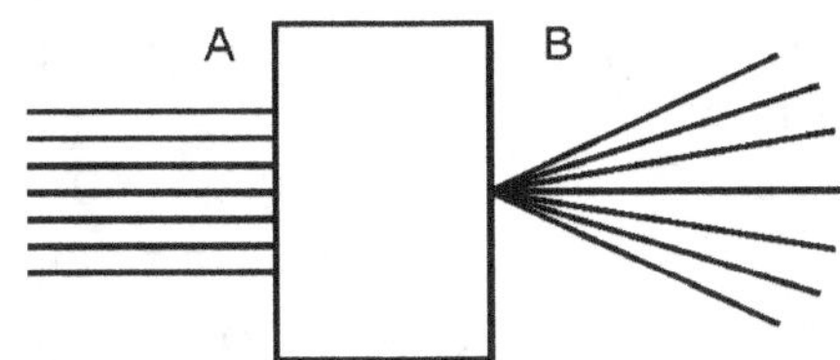


23. Which of the following statements is true?
(A) A convex lens has –4 dioptre power having a focal length 0.25 m
(B) A concave lens has 4 dioptre power having a focal length 0.50 m
(C) A concave lens has –4 dioptre power having a focal length 0.25 m
(D) A convex lens has 4 dioptre power having a focal length 0.25 m

24. Magnification produced by a rear view mirror fitted in which lens is ____________.
(A) Less than one
(B) More than one
(C) Equal to one
(D) Can be more or less than one depending upon the position of the object in front of it.

25. A full length image of a distant tall building can definitely be seen by using ____________.
(A) A concave mirror
(B) A convex mirror
(C) A plane mirror
(D) Both concave as well as plane mirror

26. In torches, search lights and headlights of vehicles, the bulb is placed ____________.
(A) Very near to the focus of the reflector
(B) Between the pole and the focus of the reflector
(C) At the centre of curvature of the reflector
(D) Between the focus and centre of curvature of the reflector

27. When a ray of light is incident (coming out) from a glass slab into the air, then the reflected ray will be ____________.
(A) Near to the normal
(B) Away from the normal
(C) On the same path of the normal
(D) Reflected back in the glass slab

28. Which of the following has a very high refractive index?
(A) Water
(B) Ice
(C) Diamond
(D) Crown glass

29. You are given water, mustard oil, glycerine and kerosene. In which of these media a ray of light incident obliquely at same angle would bend the most?
(A) Kerosene
(B) Water
(C) Mustard oil
(D) Glycerine

30. Which of the following ray diagrams is correct for the ray of light incident on a concave mirror?

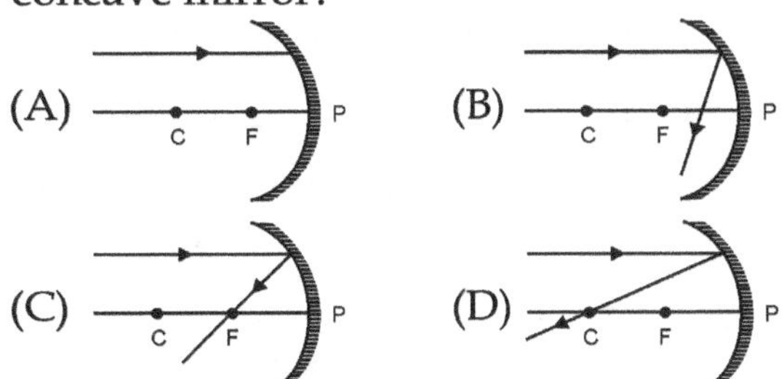

31. An erect image, 3 times the size of the object is obtained with a concave mirror of radius of curvature 36 cm. What is the position of the object 'u' from the mirror?

    (A) –10 cm      (B) –12 cm
    (C) 12 cm      (D) –6 cm

32. The linear magnification produced by a convex mirror is always positive. This is because ___________.

    (A) The image formed by a convex mirror is always virtual and erect.
    (B) The image formed by a convex mirror is always smaller in size than the object.
    (C) The convex mirror is a small mirror.
    (D) The image formed by a convex mirror is real.

33. How much time will light take to cross 2 mm thick glass pane if refractive index of glass is $\dfrac{3}{2}$?

    (A) $10^{-7}$ s      (B) $10^{-8}$ s
    (C) $10^{-10}$ s      (D) $10^{-11}$ s

34. A ray of light falling normally on a mirror retraces its path on reflection. This is because ___________.

    (A) $\angle i = 90°$      (B) $\angle i = 0°$
    (C) $\angle i = 45°$      (D) none of these

35. A ray of light falls on one face of an equilateral glass prism at 40° and emerges from the face at the same angle. The deviation suffered by the ray is ___________.

    (A) 20°      (B) 40°
    (C) 60°      (D) 80°

---

—Darken Your Choice with HB Pencil—

| | | | | | | | | | | | | | | | |
|---|---|---|---|---|---|---|---|---|---|---|---|---|---|---|---|
| 1. | Ⓐ Ⓑ Ⓒ Ⓓ | 8. | Ⓐ Ⓑ Ⓒ Ⓓ | 15. | Ⓐ Ⓑ Ⓒ Ⓓ | 22 | Ⓐ Ⓑ Ⓒ Ⓓ | 29. | Ⓐ Ⓑ Ⓒ Ⓓ |
| 2. | Ⓐ Ⓑ Ⓒ Ⓓ | 9. | Ⓐ Ⓑ Ⓒ Ⓓ | 16. | Ⓐ Ⓑ Ⓒ Ⓓ | 23. | Ⓐ Ⓑ Ⓒ Ⓓ | 30. | Ⓐ Ⓑ Ⓒ Ⓓ |
| 3. | Ⓐ Ⓑ Ⓒ Ⓓ | 10. | Ⓐ Ⓑ Ⓒ Ⓓ | 17. | Ⓐ Ⓑ Ⓒ Ⓓ | 24. | Ⓐ Ⓑ Ⓒ Ⓓ | 31. | Ⓐ Ⓑ Ⓒ Ⓓ |
| 4. | Ⓐ Ⓑ Ⓒ Ⓓ | 11. | Ⓐ Ⓑ Ⓒ Ⓓ | 18. | Ⓐ Ⓑ Ⓒ Ⓓ | 25. | Ⓐ Ⓑ Ⓒ Ⓓ | 32. | Ⓐ Ⓑ Ⓒ Ⓓ |
| 5. | Ⓐ Ⓑ Ⓒ Ⓓ | 12. | Ⓐ Ⓑ Ⓒ Ⓓ | 19. | Ⓐ Ⓑ Ⓒ Ⓓ | 26. | Ⓐ Ⓑ Ⓒ Ⓓ | 33. | Ⓐ Ⓑ Ⓒ Ⓓ |
| 6. | Ⓐ Ⓑ Ⓒ Ⓓ | 13. | Ⓐ Ⓑ Ⓒ Ⓓ | 20. | Ⓐ Ⓑ Ⓒ Ⓓ | 27. | Ⓐ Ⓑ Ⓒ Ⓓ | 34. | Ⓐ Ⓑ Ⓒ Ⓓ |
| 7. | Ⓐ Ⓑ Ⓒ Ⓓ | 14. | Ⓐ Ⓑ Ⓒ Ⓓ | 21. | Ⓐ Ⓑ Ⓒ Ⓓ | 28. | Ⓐ Ⓑ Ⓒ Ⓓ | 35. | Ⓐ Ⓑ Ⓒ Ⓓ |

# HUMAN EYE AND COLOURFUL WORLD

## LEARNING OBJECTIVES

➤ Human eye and its working

➤ The power of accommodation of human eye

➤ Refraction of light through prism

## MULTIPLE CHOICE QUESTIONS

1. The change in focal length of an eye lens to focus the image of the objects at varying distances is done by the action of __________.
   (A) Retina
   (B) Ciliary muscles
   (C) Iris
   (D) Pupil

2. The splitting up of the light into its constituent colours, and the coloured bands so obtained on the screen are called __________.
   (A) Dispersion (B) Scattering
   (C) Spectrum (D) Refraction

3. The cells which enable us to distinguish between different colours are __________.
   (A) Rod shaped
   (B) Cone shaped
   (C) Both types of cells
   (D) None of these

4. The property of eye which is used in cinematography is __________.
   (A) Persistence of vision
   (B) Power of accommodation
   (C) Colour blindness
   (D) Range of vision

5. Cataract is a flow that arises when eye lens of person becomes __________.
   (A) Hazy (opaque) (B) Transparent
   (C) Black (D) None of these

6. The essential condition for Rayleigh's elastic scattering is __________.
   (A) Size of scatterer (x) must be much less then the wavelength of light ($\lambda$) incident *i.e.*, $x \ll \lambda$
   (B) $x \gg \lambda$
   (C) $x = \lambda$
   (D) independent of x and $\lambda$

7. The deviation of a ray of light passing through a prism depends on __________.
   (A) Angle of prism
   (B) Nature of material of the prism
   (C) Angle of incidence of the ray
   (D) All of these

8. The longest visible wavelength 800.0 Å is of __________ colour.
   (A) Violet (B) Red
   (C) Green (D) Orange

9. What is the frequency of violet colour of wavelength 4000 Å?
   (A) $3.5 \times 10^{14}$ Hz (B) $3.75 \times 10^{14}$ Hz
   (C) $7.5 \times 10^{14}$ Hz (D) $7.25 \times 10^{14}$ Hz

10. The cause of advanced sunrise and delayed sunset is ____________.
    (A) Scattering of sunlight
    (B) Dispersion
    (C) Atmospheric refraction
    (D) None of these

11. Blue colour of clear sky is on account of ____________.
    (A) Scattering of sunlight
    (B) Dispersion
    (C) Atmospheric refraction
    (D) None of these

12. The intensity of scattered light ($I_s$) varies inversely as the ____________ power of wavelength ($\lambda$).
    (A) First          (B) Second
    (C) Third          (D) Fourth

13. The intensity of scattered violet light is ____________ times the intensity of scattered red light.
    (A) Four           (B) Eight
    (C) Sixteen        (D) Two

14. How many times does a ray of light bend on passing through prism?
    (A) Once           (B) Twice
    (C) Thrice         (D) Four times

15. The visible part of electromagnetic spectrum lies in between ____________.
    (A) Ultraviolet and infrared rays
    (B) Infrared and microwave rays
    (C) X-ray and infrared rays
    (D) X-ray and gamma rays

16. The refractive index of glass is 3/2. Velocity of light in glass would be ____________.
    (A) $3 \times 10^8$ m/s
    (B) $2 \times 10^8$ m/s
    (C) $10^8$ m/s
    (D) $1.33 \times 10^8$ m/s

17. A student sitting on the last bench can read the letters written on the blackboard but is unable to read from his textbook. Which of the following statements is correct?
    (A) The near point A his eyes has receded away
    (B) The near point A his eyes has closer to him
    (C) The far point A his eyes has closed to him
    (D) The far point A his eyes has receded away

18. At noon, the sun appears white as ____________.
    (A) Blue colour is scattered the most
    (B) Red colour is scattered the most
    (C) All the colours of white light are scattered away
    (D) Light is least scattered

19. If a body appears red colour in red light, the real colour of the body is ____________.
    (A) Definitely white
    (B) Definitely red
    (C) Either red or white
    (D) Any colour except red and white

20. Which of the following phenomena of light are involved in formation of a rainbow?
    (A) Reflection, refraction and dispersion
    (B) Refraction, dispersion and total internal reflection
    (C) Refraction, dispersion and internal reflection
    (D) Dispersion, scattering and total internal reflection

21. Which of the following contributes significantly to the reddish appearance of the sun at sunrise and sunset?
    (A) Scattering of light
    (B) Dispersion of light
    (C) Total internal reflection of light
    (D) Reflection of light from the earth

22. The bluish colour of water in deep sea is due to ____________.
    (A) The presence of algae in water
    (B) Reflection of sky in water

(C) Scattering of light

(D) Absorption of light by the sea

23. When light rays enter the eye, most of the refraction occurs on the _____________.

(A) Iris

(B) Pupil

(C) Outer surface of the cornea

(D) Crystalline lens

24. The focal length of eye lens increases when eye muscles _____________.

(A) Are released and lens becomes thinner

(B) Contract and lens becomes thicker

(C) Are released and lens becomes thicker

(D) Contract and lens becomes thinner

25. A glass prism has _____________.

(A) Six rectangular surfaces

(B) Four rectangular surfaces

(C) Two triangular bases and their rectangular surfaces

(D) None of these

26. For which defect of vision cylindrical lenses are used?

(A) Myopia      (B) Astigmatism

(C) Hypermetropia      (D) Presbyopia

27. If A is angle of prism D is an angle of deviation, I is angle of incidence and E is the angle of emergence through a prism, then the correct relation between the four angles is _____________.

(A) $A + I = D + E$

(B) $A + D = I + E$

(C) $A + E = D + I$

(D) $A + I + E = D$

28. Angle of deviation through a prism of angle 60°, when angles of incidence and emergence are 40° each is _____________.

(A) 40°      (B) 20°

(C) 60°      (D) 30°

29. Dispersion of light through a prism is _____________.

(A) Same as reflection

(B) Same as refraction

(C) Splitting of white light into its constituent colours

(D) None of these

30. _____________ is at the lower end and _____________ is at the upper end of the visible spectrum.

(A) Violet, red      (B) Red, blue

(C) Red, violet      (D) Blue, red

## HOTS (ACHIEVERS SECTION)

31. The front transparent part of the eye which is bulged outwards is called _____________.

(A) Cornea      (B) Vitreous body

(C) Pupil      (D) Iris

32. Which of the following is not true?

(A) Iris decides the colour of the eye.

(B) The hole in the centre of cornea is called conjunctiva.

(C) Retina acts like a screen for the image formation in eye

(D) None of these

33. **Statement 1:** The focal length or converging power of eye lens is not fixed.

**Statement 2:** Ciliary muscles can modify the curvature of eye lens to some extent.

(A) Statement 1 is true but statement 2 is false.

(B) Statement 2 is true but statement 1 is false

(C) Both statement 1 and statement 2 are true but statement 2 is not the reason for statement 1.

(D) Both statement 1 and statement 2 are true and statement 2 is the reason for statement 1.

34. The ability of eye lens to adjust its focal length to form a sharp image of the object at varying distances on the retina is called

    (A) Power of observation of the eye

    (B) Power of adjustment of the eye

    (C) Power of accommodation of the eye

    (D) Power of enabling of the eye

35. The defective eye of a person has near point 0.5 m and point 3 m. The power far corrective lens required for (i) reading purpose and (ii) seeing distant objects, respectively are:

    (A) 0.5 D and +3 D

    (B) +2 D and −0.33 D

    (C) −2 D and +0.33 D

    (D) 0.5 D and −3.0 D

---

Darken Your Choice with HB Pencil

| 1. | Ⓐ Ⓑ Ⓒ Ⓓ | 8. | Ⓐ Ⓑ Ⓒ Ⓓ | 15. | Ⓐ Ⓑ Ⓒ Ⓓ | 22 | Ⓐ Ⓑ Ⓒ Ⓓ | 29. | Ⓐ Ⓑ Ⓒ Ⓓ |
| 2. | Ⓐ Ⓑ Ⓒ Ⓓ | 9. | Ⓐ Ⓑ Ⓒ Ⓓ | 16. | Ⓐ Ⓑ Ⓒ Ⓓ | 23. | Ⓐ Ⓑ Ⓒ Ⓓ | 30. | Ⓐ Ⓑ Ⓒ Ⓓ |
| 3. | Ⓐ Ⓑ Ⓒ Ⓓ | 10. | Ⓐ Ⓑ Ⓒ Ⓓ | 17. | Ⓐ Ⓑ Ⓒ Ⓓ | 24. | Ⓐ Ⓑ Ⓒ Ⓓ | 31. | Ⓐ Ⓑ Ⓒ Ⓓ |
| 4. | Ⓐ Ⓑ Ⓒ Ⓓ | 11. | Ⓐ Ⓑ Ⓒ Ⓓ | 18. | Ⓐ Ⓑ Ⓒ Ⓓ | 25. | Ⓐ Ⓑ Ⓒ Ⓓ | 32. | Ⓐ Ⓑ Ⓒ Ⓓ |
| 5. | Ⓐ Ⓑ Ⓒ Ⓓ | 12. | Ⓐ Ⓑ Ⓒ Ⓓ | 19. | Ⓐ Ⓑ Ⓒ Ⓓ | 26. | Ⓐ Ⓑ Ⓒ Ⓓ | 33. | Ⓐ Ⓑ Ⓒ Ⓓ |
| 6. | Ⓐ Ⓑ Ⓒ Ⓓ | 13. | Ⓐ Ⓑ Ⓒ Ⓓ | 20. | Ⓐ Ⓑ Ⓒ Ⓓ | 27. | Ⓐ Ⓑ Ⓒ Ⓓ | 34. | Ⓐ Ⓑ Ⓒ Ⓓ |
| 7. | Ⓐ Ⓑ Ⓒ Ⓓ | 14. | Ⓐ Ⓑ Ⓒ Ⓓ | 21. | Ⓐ Ⓑ Ⓒ Ⓓ | 28. | Ⓐ Ⓑ Ⓒ Ⓓ | 35. | Ⓐ Ⓑ Ⓒ Ⓓ |

# ELECTRICITY

## LEARNING OBJECTIVES

➤ Electric current and electric circuit

➤ Potential difference and Ohm,'s Law

➤ Resistance and factors affecting resistance

➤ The combination of resistors in series and parallel

## MULTIPLE CHOICE QUESTIONS

1. If two copper wires of length $l$ and $2l$, area A and 2A are taken, then —————.
   - (A) The specific resistance of first is greater than that of the second
   - (B) The specific resistance of the second wire is greater than that of the first
   - (C) The specific resistance of both the wires is same
   - (D) The specific resistance is not be predictable

2. A circuit has a fuse of 5 A. What is the maximum number of 100 W (220 V) bulbs, can be safely used in this circuit?
   - (A) 11       (B) 14
   - (C) 15       (D) 20

3. Find the amount of the energy given to 5 coulombs of charge passing through a 10 volt battery.
   - (A) 20 J       (B) 25 J
   - (C) 50 J       (D) 100 J

4. The flow of electric current can be compared to that of water flow because current flows from —————.
   - (A) Higher potential to lower potential
   - (B) Higher resistance to lower resistance
   - (C) Higher potential energy to lower potential energy
   - (D) Any direction of the circuit

5. If equal resistances of 5 Ω each are connected in parallel with a battery, then —————.
   - (A) The total resistance is also 5 Ω
   - (B) The current flowing in each resistor will be same
   - (C) The potential difference across each resistance is not same
   - (D) None of these

6. Calculate the equivalent resistance of the circuit shown below —————.

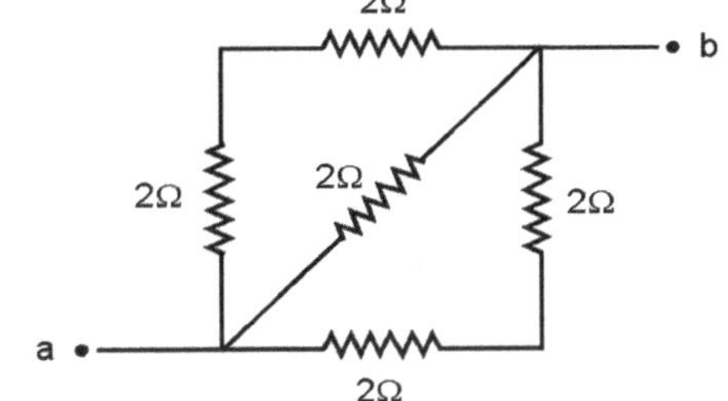



   - (A) 1 Ω       (B) 2 Ω
   - (C) 6 Ω       (D) 8 Ω

7. What happens to the overall current of the electric circuit in parallel connection when the power supply from the source is lowered?
   - (A) Increase
   - (B) Decreases
   - (C) No change
   - (D) Can't be determined

8. How much work is done in moving a charge of 5 C from a point in circuit at 220 volts to another point at 240 volts?

(A) 50 Joules

(B) 100 Joules

(C) 125 Joules

(D) 250 Joules

9. If the potential difference across the ends of a conductor is doubled, what will be the effect on the current flowing through it?

(A) It gets doubled

(B) It gets halved

(C) It remains same

(D) None of these

10. What is the total current flowing in this circuit?

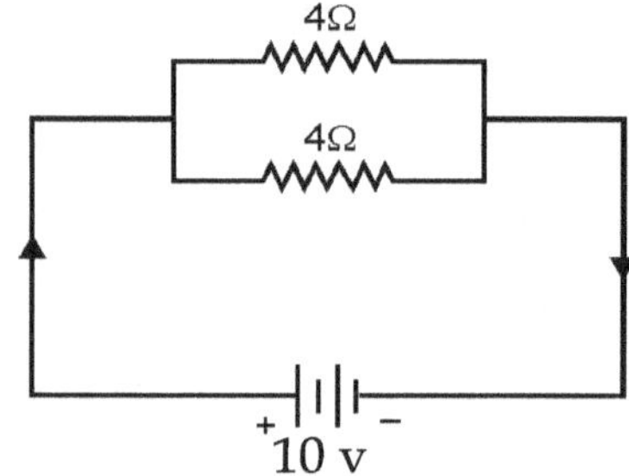

(A) 2 A  (B) 0.5 A

(C) 10 A  (D) 5 A

11. What does this graph with straight line OA represents?

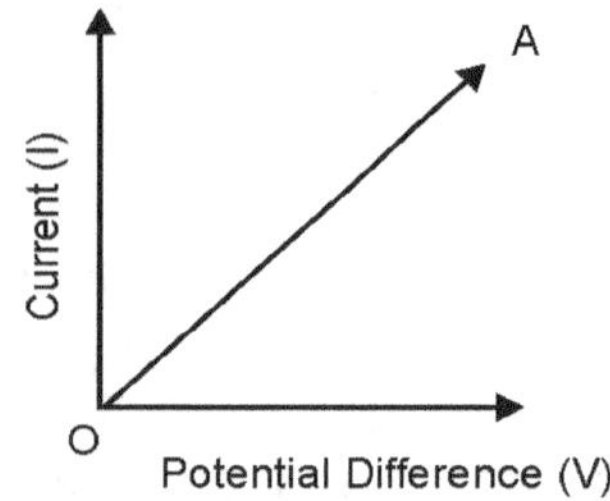

(A) V is directly proportional to I

(B) V is inversely proportional to I

(C) V is independent of I

(D) V and I goes in opposite directions

12. Three resistors are connected as shown below in a closed circuit. What is the effective resistance of the whole circuit ________.

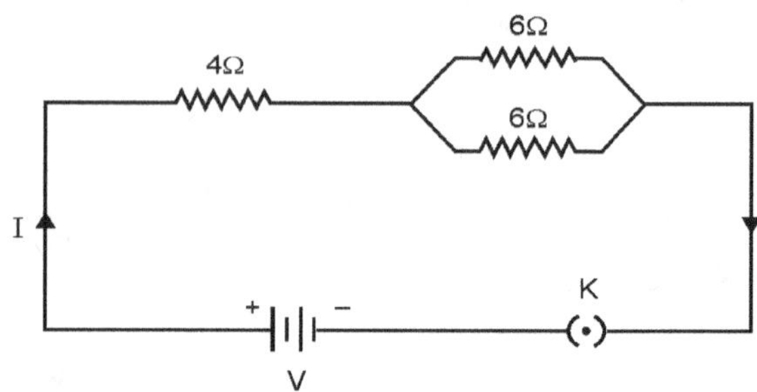

(A) 4 Ω  (B) 7 Ω

(C) 10 Ω  (D) 16 Ω

13. Identify the best conductor of electricity among the following ________.

(A) Pb  (B) Mg

(C) Ag  (D) Fe

14. The proper presentation of series combination of cells to obtain maximum potential is ________.

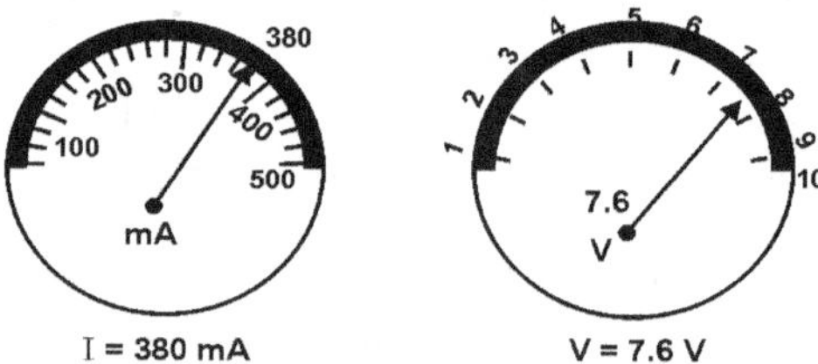

(A) Fig (i)

(B) Fig (ii)

(C) Fig (iii)

(D) None of these

15. The current flowing through a conductor and the potential difference across its two ends are as per the reading of the ammeter and the voltmeter shown below. The resistance of the conductor would be ________.

I = 380 mA    V = 7.6 V

(A) 0.02 Ω

(B) 2.00 Ω

(C) 12 Ω

(D) 20 Ω

16. The given circuit diagram shows the experimental arrangement of different circuit components for determination of equivalent resistance of two resistors $R_1$ and $R_2$ connected in series

The components X, Y and Z shown in the circuit represent —————.

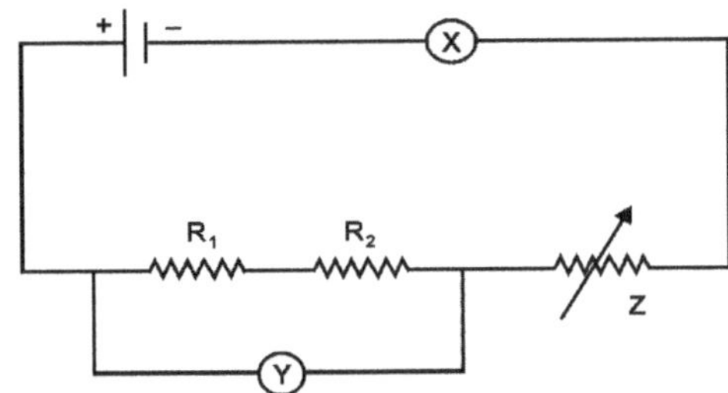

(A) Rheostat, Resistor, Ammeter
(B) Voltmeter, Ammeter, Rheostat
(C) Ammeter, Voltmeter, Rheostat
(D) Rheostat, Ammeter, Resistor

17. A multimeter is used to measure —————.

(A) Current only
(B) Resistance only
(C) Voltage only
(D) All of these

18. A number of cells when connected in series form —————.

(A) A generator
(B) A battery
(C) An inverter
(D) A circuit

19. Which of the following circuit set-ups shows the dependence of current on potential difference across a resistor (as per Ohm's Law)?

(A)
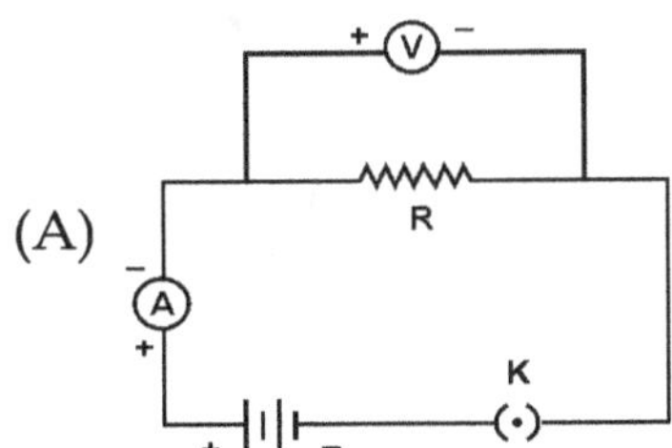

(B)
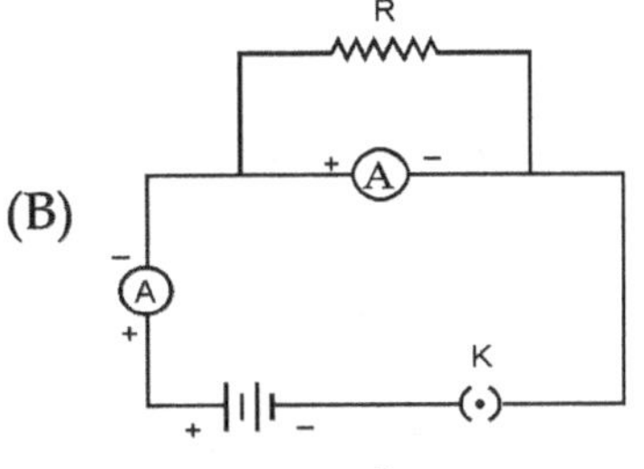

(C)
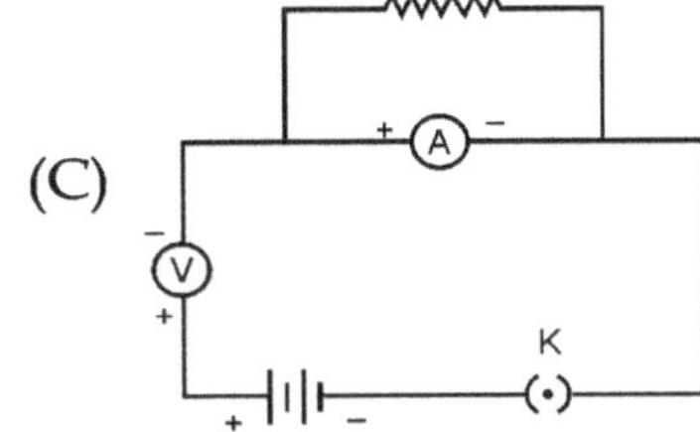

(D)
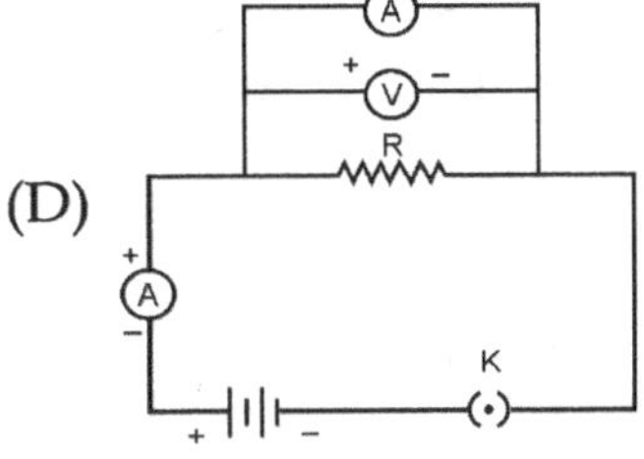

20. The resistance of a straight conductor is independent of —————.
(A) Temperature
(B) Material
(C) Cross-sectional area
(D) Shape of cross-section

21 The resistivity of a wire depends on its —————.

(A) Length
(B) Cross-sectional area
(C) Dimensions
(D) Material

22. Two wires A and B are made of silver. Both wires are 3 m long but wire A is 1 mm thick and wire B is 4 mm thick. The resistivity is —————.

(A) More for A
(B) More for B
(C) Same for A and B as both are made of same material
(D) Same for A and B as they have equal length

23. The V-I graph of three resistors A, B and C are as shown in the figure given below. Which resistor has maximum resistance?

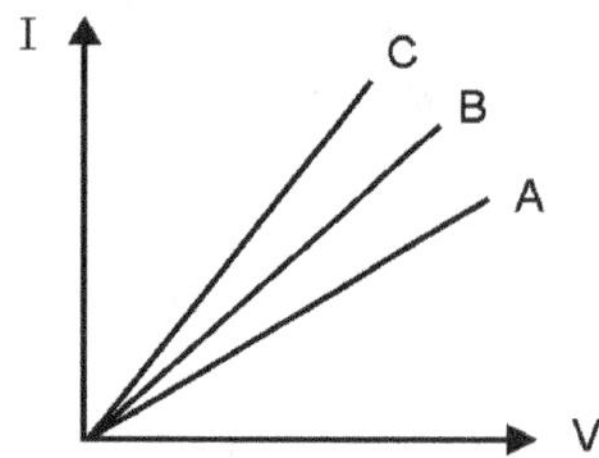

(A) A

(B) B

(C) C

(D) All three have same resistances

24. Which of the following equations does not represent Ohm's Law?

(A) Current/potential difference = constant

(B) Potential difference/current = constant

(C) Potential difference = current × resistance

(D) Current = resistance × potential difference

25. If a wire is stretched to make its length twice the present length, its resistance will become ——————.

(A) Two times

(B) Four times

(C) Eight times

(D) Remains the same

26. The current flowing through the circuit shown in the circuit is 2 A. The pd across the battery terminals is ——————.

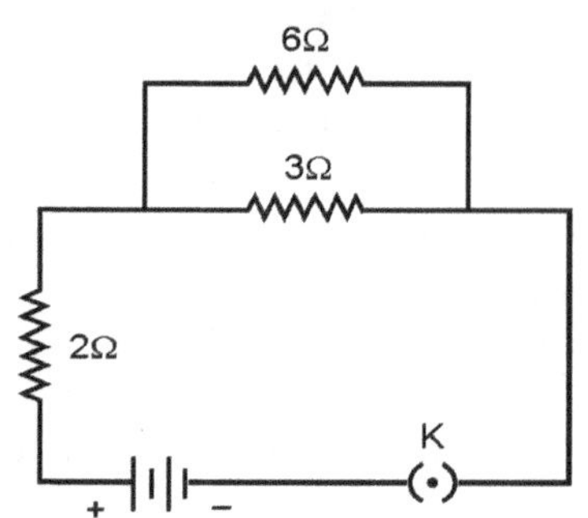

(A) 2 V      (B) 6 V

(C) 8 V      (D) 12 V

27. Two wires of same material and equal length have radii $r_1$ and $r_2$ respectively. The ratio between the two resistance $R_1$ and $R_2$ of both the wires is ——————.

(A) $\dfrac{R_1}{R_2} = \dfrac{r_1^2}{r_1^2}$

(B) $\dfrac{R_1}{R_2} = \dfrac{r_2^2}{r_1^2}$

(C) $\dfrac{R_1}{R_2} = \dfrac{r_1}{r_2}$

(D) $\dfrac{R_1}{R_2} = \dfrac{r_1}{r_2}$

28. A 60 W bulb carries a current of 0.5A. The charge that passes through it in 2 hours is ——————.

(A) 3600 C      (B) 3000 C

(C) 6000 C      (D) 1500 C

29. The resistance of an ideal ammeter and an ideal voltmeter is ——————.

(A) Infinity, infinity respectively

(B) Zero, infinity respectively

(C) Infinity, zero respectively

(D) Zero, zero respectively

30. A wire of resistance 1 Ω is divided into two halves and both halves are connected in parallel. The new resistance will be ——————.

(A) 1 Ω      (B) 0.5 Ω

(C) 0.25 Ω      (D) 2 Ω

31. The electric resistance of a certain wire of iron is R. If its length and radius are both doubled, then __________.
    (A) The resistance will be doubled and the specific resistance will be halved.
    (B) The resistance will be halved and the specific resistance will be doubled.
    (C) The resistance will be halved and the specific resistance will remain unchanged.
    (D) The resistance and the specific resistance will both remain unchanged.

32. A combination of six resistors $R_1$, $R_2$, $R_3$, $R_4$, $R_5$, and $R_6$ are shown in the figure. Find the equivalent resistance between points A and B on the circuit.
    (A) 8.25 Ω          (B) 8.0 Ω
    (C) 7.25 Ω          (D) 7.85 Ω

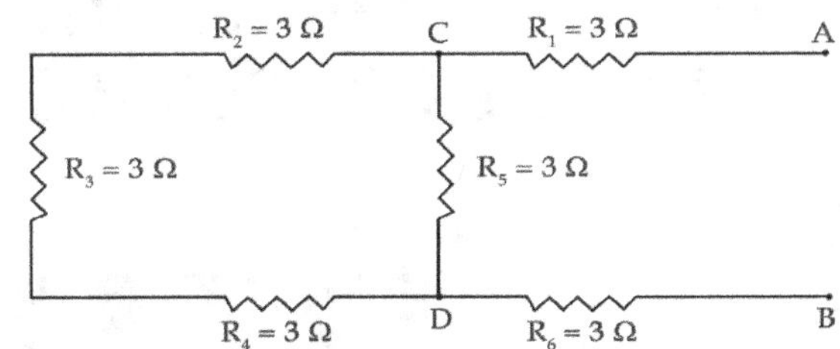


33. Heat of 100 J is produced each second in a 4 Ω resistance. The potential difference across the resistor is __________.
    (A) 200 V          (B) 20V
    (C) 40 V           (D) 220 V

34. The best conductor of electricity is __________.
    (A) Copper         (B) Silver
    (C) Aluminum       (D) None of these

35. __________ is used in making the filament of an electric bulb?
    (A) Copper         (B) Aluminium
    (C) Tungsten       (D) Silver

| | | | | | | | | | | | | | | | | | | | |
|---|---|---|---|---|---|---|---|---|---|---|---|---|---|---|---|---|---|---|---|
| 1. | Ⓐ Ⓑ Ⓒ Ⓓ | 7. | Ⓐ Ⓑ Ⓒ Ⓓ | 13. | Ⓐ Ⓑ Ⓒ Ⓓ | 19 | Ⓐ Ⓑ Ⓒ Ⓓ | 25. | Ⓐ Ⓑ Ⓒ Ⓓ |
| 2. | Ⓐ Ⓑ Ⓒ Ⓓ | 8. | Ⓐ Ⓑ Ⓒ Ⓓ | 14. | Ⓐ Ⓑ Ⓒ Ⓓ | 20. | Ⓐ Ⓑ Ⓒ Ⓓ | 26. | Ⓐ Ⓑ Ⓒ Ⓓ |
| 3. | Ⓐ Ⓑ Ⓒ Ⓓ | 9. | Ⓐ Ⓑ Ⓒ Ⓓ | 15. | Ⓐ Ⓑ Ⓒ Ⓓ | 21. | Ⓐ Ⓑ Ⓒ Ⓓ | 27. | Ⓐ Ⓑ Ⓒ Ⓓ |
| 4. | Ⓐ Ⓑ Ⓒ Ⓓ | 10. | Ⓐ Ⓑ Ⓒ Ⓓ | 16. | Ⓐ Ⓑ Ⓒ Ⓓ | 22. | Ⓐ Ⓑ Ⓒ Ⓓ | 28. | Ⓐ Ⓑ Ⓒ Ⓓ |
| 5. | Ⓐ Ⓑ Ⓒ Ⓓ | 11. | Ⓐ Ⓑ Ⓒ Ⓓ | 17. | Ⓐ Ⓑ Ⓒ Ⓓ | 23. | Ⓐ Ⓑ Ⓒ Ⓓ | 29. | Ⓐ Ⓑ Ⓒ Ⓓ |
| 6. | Ⓐ Ⓑ Ⓒ Ⓓ | 12. | Ⓐ Ⓑ Ⓒ Ⓓ | 18. | Ⓐ Ⓑ Ⓒ Ⓓ | 24. | Ⓐ Ⓑ Ⓒ Ⓓ | 30. | Ⓐ Ⓑ Ⓒ Ⓓ |

# MAGNETIC EFFECTS OF ELECTRIC CURRENT

## LEARNING OBJECTIVES

➤ Magnetic field and field lines
➤ Magnetic field due to a current carrying conductor
➤ Magnetic field due to a current carrying solenoid
➤ Electromagnetic Induction

## MULTIPLE CHOICE QUESTIONS

1. At the time of short circuit, the current in the circuit __________.
   (A) Reduces substantially
   (B) Does not change
   (C) Increase heavily
   (D) Vary continuously

2. What type of material is used in the core of an electromagnet?
   (A) Soft iron      (B) Steel
   (C) Alloy      (D) Non-metal

3. A straight wire of mass 200 g and length 1.5 m carries a current of 2A. It is suspended in mid air by a uniform horizontal magnetic field whose magnitude in Tesla is __________.
   (A) 2 T      (B) 0.65 T
   (C) 1.3 T      (D) 0.55 T

4. Which of these factors affect(s) the strength of an electromagnet?
   (A) The number of turns in a coil
   (B) The current flowing in the coil
   (C) The length of gap between its poles
   (D) All of these

5. The magnetic field at a distance of 10 cm from a long wire carrying current is 2 tesla. The magnetic field at a distance of 20 cm is __________.

   (A) 0.5 T      (B) 1 T
   (C) 1.5 T      (D) 2 T

6. A straight wire of diameter 2.5 mm carrying a current of 2 A is replaced by another thick wire of 5 mm diameter. The strength of the magnetic field far away is __________.
   (A) Twice the earlier value
   (B) One-half of the earlier value
   (C) One-quarter of the earlier value
   (D) Same as the earlier value

7. A long solenoid carrying a current produces a magnetic field B along its axis. If the current is doubled and the number of turns per cm is halved, then the new value of magnetic field is __________.
   (A) $\dfrac{B}{2}$      (B) B
   (C) 2 B      (D) 4 B

8. Match the following.

   (i) Magnetic field due to a current carrying straight conductor    a. $B \propto nI$

   (ii) Magnetic field due to a solenoid    b. $B \propto \dfrac{IN}{r}$

   (iii) Magnetic field due to circular coil carrying current    c. $B \propto \dfrac{I}{r}$

(A) (i) – b, (ii) – a, (iii) – c
(B) (i) – c, (ii) – b, (iii) – a
(C) (i) – c, (ii) – a, (iii) – b
(D) (i) – a, (ii) – b, (iii) – c

9. Match the following.

(i) Force acting on a charged particle (q) moving with velocity V in a magnetic field. B in direction perpendicular to the direction of B.    a. 0

(ii) Force acting on a charged particle (q) moving in a magnetic field B in a direction parallel to it.    b. $(F = IlB)$

(iii) Force acting on a conductor when it is placed perpendicular to the direction of B.    c. $F = qvB$

(A) (i) – c, (ii) – a, (iii) – b
(B) (i) – a, (ii) – b, (iii) – c
(C) (i) – c, (ii) – b, (iii) – a
(D) (i) – b, (ii) – c, (iii) – a

10. Permanent magnets are made up of __________.

(A) Ferronite (alloy of Fe, Ni and Mg)
(B) Alnico (alloy of Al, Ni and Co)
(C) Iron ore
(D) Bauxite ore

11. In case of a current-carrying circular coil, the magnetic field is maximum __________.

(A) At its centre
(B) At the ends of the coil
(C) Any where inside the coil
(D) Outside the coil

12. To which wire amongst the following, an electric fuse connected?

(A) Neutral
(B) Earth
(C) Live
(D) None of these

13. What material is used to make a fuse wire?

(A) Alloy of Ni, Al, and Co
(B) Alloy of Fe, Cu and Ni
(C) Alloy of Pb and Sn
(D) Alloy of Pb and Fe

14. Which polarity is developed on the face of the solenoid when a north pole of a magnet is moving towards it?

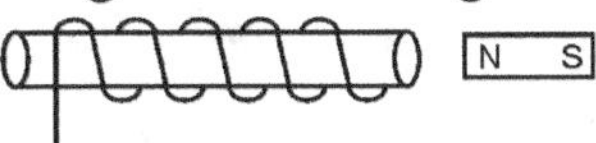

(A) North pole      (B) South pole
(C) Neutral      (D) Can't be found

15. An AC of frequency 50 Hz changes its polarity after every __________.

(A) $\dfrac{1}{25}$ second      (B) $\dfrac{1}{50}$ second

(C) $\dfrac{1}{75}$ second      (D) $\dfrac{1}{100}$ second

16. The rate of change of flux is greater in case when a magnet is moved towards a coil __________.

(A) Very quickly
(B) Very slowly
(C) Moderately
(D) No change

17. An induced emf is produced when a magnet is plunged into a coil. The magnetic field of induced emf does not depend on __________.

(A) The number of turns in the coil
(B) The speed with which the magnet is moved
(C) The strength of the magnet
(D) The resistivity of the material of the coil

18. A dynamo __________.

(A) Creates electrical energy
(B) Creates mechanical energy
(C) Converts mechanical energy into electrical energy
(D) Converts electrical energy into mechanical energy

19. An electric bulb rated 220 V is connected to 220 V, 5 Hz AC source. The bulb __________.
   (A) Does not glow
   (B) Glows immediately
   (C) Glows continuously
   (D) Gets fused

20. The magnitude of induced emf in a generator can be increased __________.
   (A) By increasing the speed of rotation of the coil
   (B) By increasing the area of the armature and number of the turns in the armature
   (C) By increasing the strength of the magnetic field in which the coil rotates
   (D) All of these

21. Which of these fact(s) is TRUE?
   (A) AC is more dangerous than DC as it attracts a person
   (B) AC cannot be used for electroplating, electrotyping and other such electrolytic processes
   (C) The power wastage in AC transmission is negligible as compared to DC
   (D) All of these

22. The magnetic field inside a long straight solenoid carrying current __________.
   (A) Is zero
   (B) Decreases as we move towards its end
   (C) Increasing as we move towards its end
   (D) Is uniform at all points

23. Commercial electric motors do not use __________.
   (A) An electromagnet to rotate the armature
   (B) Effectively large number of turns of conducting wire in the current-carrying coil
   (C) A permanent magnet to rotate the armature
   (D) A soft iron core on which the coil is wound

24. What is the potential difference of current in Indian household circuit ?
   (A) 220 V      (B) 240 V
   (C) 330 V      (D) 440 V

25. Which one of the following helps in changing the directions of current in AC generator?
   (A) Carbon brush
   (B) Spilt rings
   (C) Coil armature
   (D) Slip rings

26. What is the current rating of power switch current in our household circuit?
   (A) 5 A      (B) 10 A
   (C) 15 A      (D) 20 A

27. The most important safety method used for protecting home appliances from short-circuiting or overloading is __________.
   (A) Earthing
   (B) Use of fuse
   (C) Use of stabilisers
   (D) Use of the electric meter

28. What are permanent magnets made of?
   (A) Steel      (B) Alnico
   (C) Nipermag      (D) All of these

29. The two types of circuits used to run domestic appliances are __________.
   (A) 5 A and 15 A      (B) 20 A and 5 A
   (C) 25A and 15 A      (D) 5 A and 10 A

30. A rectangular coil of copper wires is rotated in a magnetic field. The direction of the induced current changes once in each __________.
   (A) Two revolutions
   (B) One revolution
   (C) Half revolution
   (D) One-fourth of revolution

31. An induced emf is produced when a magnet is plunged into a coil. The magnitude of induced emf does not depend on __________.
    (A) The number of turns in the coil
    (B) The resistivity of the material of the coil
    (C) The speed with which the magnet is moved
    (D) The strength of the magnet.

32. Which of the following statements is NOT true?
    (A) The relative strength of magnetic field is shown by the degree of closeness of the field lines.
    (B) Magnetic field lines are closed curves.
    (C) The direction of magnetic field at a point is taken to be the direction in which the north pole of the magnet compass needle points.
    (D) If magnetic field lines are parallel and equidistant, they represent zero field strength.

33. **Statement 1:** Magnetic field lines are widely spaced near the poles and denser near the centre.
    **Statement 2:** Magnetic field lines always emerge from north pole and converge at south pole.

(A) Statement 1 is true but statement 2 is false.
(B) Statement 2 is true but statement 1 is false.
(C) Both statements 1 and statement 2 are true but statement 2 is not the reason of statement 1.
(D) Both statement 1 and statement 2 are true and statement 2 is the correct reason for statement 1.

34. Which of the labelling in the given figure shows the direction of the current using Fleming's Left-Hand Rule?

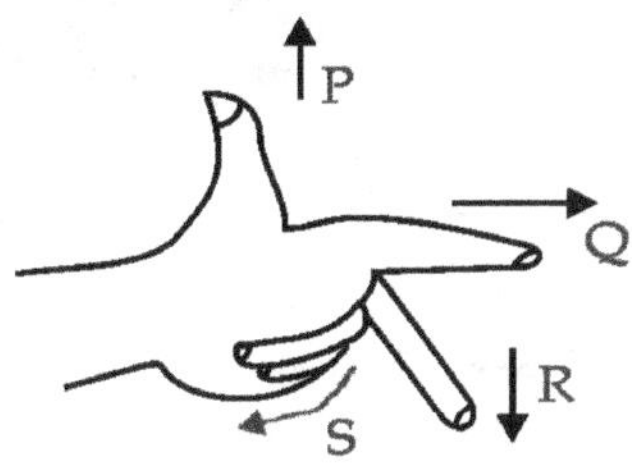


(A) P      (B) Q
(C) R      (D) S

35. The force exerted on a current-carrying wire placed in a magnetic field is zero when the angle between the wire and the direction of the magnetic field is __________.
(A) 180 degree      (B) 45 degree
(C) 90 degree      (D) 60 degree

| 1. | Ⓐ Ⓑ Ⓒ Ⓓ | 8. | Ⓐ Ⓑ Ⓒ Ⓓ | 15. | Ⓐ Ⓑ Ⓒ Ⓓ | 22 | Ⓐ Ⓑ Ⓒ Ⓓ | 29. | Ⓐ Ⓑ Ⓒ Ⓓ |
| 2. | Ⓐ Ⓑ Ⓒ Ⓓ | 9. | Ⓐ Ⓑ Ⓒ Ⓓ | 16. | Ⓐ Ⓑ Ⓒ Ⓓ | 23. | Ⓐ Ⓑ Ⓒ Ⓓ | 30. | Ⓐ Ⓑ Ⓒ Ⓓ |
| 3. | Ⓐ Ⓑ Ⓒ Ⓓ | 10. | Ⓐ Ⓑ Ⓒ Ⓓ | 17. | Ⓐ Ⓑ Ⓒ Ⓓ | 24. | Ⓐ Ⓑ Ⓒ Ⓓ | 31. | Ⓐ Ⓑ Ⓒ Ⓓ |
| 4. | Ⓐ Ⓑ Ⓒ Ⓓ | 11. | Ⓐ Ⓑ Ⓒ Ⓓ | 18. | Ⓐ Ⓑ Ⓒ Ⓓ | 25. | Ⓐ Ⓑ Ⓒ Ⓓ | 32. | Ⓐ Ⓑ Ⓒ Ⓓ |
| 5. | Ⓐ Ⓑ Ⓒ Ⓓ | 12. | Ⓐ Ⓑ Ⓒ Ⓓ | 19. | Ⓐ Ⓑ Ⓒ Ⓓ | 26. | Ⓐ Ⓑ Ⓒ Ⓓ | 33. | Ⓐ Ⓑ Ⓒ Ⓓ |
| 6. | Ⓐ Ⓑ Ⓒ Ⓓ | 13. | Ⓐ Ⓑ Ⓒ Ⓓ | 20. | Ⓐ Ⓑ Ⓒ Ⓓ | 27. | Ⓐ Ⓑ Ⓒ Ⓓ | 34. | Ⓐ Ⓑ Ⓒ Ⓓ |
| 7. | Ⓐ Ⓑ Ⓒ Ⓓ | 14. | Ⓐ Ⓑ Ⓒ Ⓓ | 21. | Ⓐ Ⓑ Ⓒ Ⓓ | 28. | Ⓐ Ⓑ Ⓒ Ⓓ | 35. | Ⓐ Ⓑ Ⓒ Ⓓ |

# SOURCES OF ENERGY

## LEARNING OBJECTIVES

➤ The sources of energy and list their properties
➤ Fossil fuels like (coal, petroleum, LPG)
➤ The working of thermal and hydro power plant
➤ Biomass and bioenergy

## MULTIPLE CHOICE QUESTIONS

1. Which one of these is not renewable source of energy?
   (A) Solar energy
   (B) Geothermal energy
   (C) Biomass energy
   (D) Natural gas

2. Which one of these is not the conventional source of energy?
   (A) Fossil fuel
   (B) Solar energy
   (C) Biomass energy
   (D) Hydro energy

3. Which of the following is/are non-conventional source(s) of energy?
   (A) Geothermal energy
   (B) Solar energy
   (C) Ocean thermal energy
   (D) All of these

4. Which country is called 'the country of winds'?
   (A) Denmark        (B) Newzealand
   (C) Iceland        (D) India

5. Which of the following is used as a fuel at nuclear power plant?
   (A) Graphite       (B) Uranium
   (C) Hydrogen       (D) Radium

6. Which of the following agent decomposes animal wastes into biogas?
   (A) Fungus
   (B) Aerobic bacteria
   (C) Anaerobic bacteria
   (D) Virus

7. Which one is the cleanest of all these fuels?
   (A) Coke           (B) Biogas
   (C) Natural gas    (D) Kerosene

8. Is wood a renewable source of energy?
   (A) Yes
   (B) No
   (C) Cant' be said
   (D) Sometime yes

9. Aviation fuels is a special grade __________.
   (A) Natural gas
   (B) Gasoline
   (C) Petroleum
   (D) Kerosene oil

10. Decomposition of domestic wastes under natural process is known as __________.
    (A) Anaerobic fertilisation
    (B) Biodegradable process
    (C) Non-biodegradable process
    (D) Fractional distillation

11. A strong smelling agent which is added to LPG cylinders to detect gas leakage is __________.
    (A) Ethyl alcohol
    (B) Ethyl acetate
    (C) Ethyl mercaptan
    (D) Ethyl dichromate

12. The gas which is commonly found in incomplete combustion of fossil fuels is __________.
    (A) Ammonia
    (B) Carbon Monoxide
    (C) Carbon dioxide
    (D) Nitrogen

13. The process that forms the basis of hydrogen bomb is __________.
    (A) Nuclear fusion
    (B) Nuclear fission
    (C) Both (A) and (B)
    (D) Either (A) or (B)

14. The gas that leaked out during Bhopal Gas Tragedy was __________.
    (A) Carbon Monoxide
    (B) Butyle Acetate
    (C) Hydrogen Peroxide
    (D) Methyl Isocyanide

15. Hydrogen gas has high calorific value but it is not used as domestic fuel because __________.
    (A) It is highly combustible
    (B) Its production cost is high
    (C) Its transporation is difficult
    (D) All of these

16. Which one of these substances is obtained as one of the fractions during the fractional distillation of petroleum?
    (A) Coal          (B) Gasoline
    (C) Acetyline     (D) Natural gas

17. Name the product obtained by fractional distillation of petroleum which is used as a furnace fuel in metallurgical operation?
    (A) Diesel oil    (B) Gasoline
    (C) Fuel oil      (D) Petroleum gas

18. Scientists consider _____ as the fuel of future.
    (A) CNG
    (B) Hydrogen
    (C) Wave energy
    (D) Gasohol

19. Tough charcoal is a better fuel than wood and coal, it cannot be used to meet large scale requirements as __________.
    (A) It causes pollution
    (B) Its calorific value is less
    (C) It cannot be stored easily
    (D) It is not economical to use

20. Fuels which are manufactured by chemical process using primary fuels are called __________.
    (A) Secondary fuels
    (B) Industrial fuels
    (C) Clean fuels
    (D) None of these

21. Which one of these is secondary fuel?
    (A) Coke
    (B) LPG
    (C) Both (A) and (B)
    (D) None of these

22. A solar photovoltaic cell is made of __________.
    (A) A semi-conducting material
    (B) A conducting material
    (C) An alloy
    (D) An insulating material

23. The main limitation of generating nuclear energy through nuclear fission is __________.
    (A) Splitting the nucleus
    (B) Converting nuclear energy into electric energy
    (C) Sustaining chain reaction
    (D) Disposal of nuclear wastes

24. Wind power of a windmill is __________.
    (A) Directly proportional to the square of the wind speed
    (B) Directly proportional to the cube of the wind speed

(C) Directly proportional to the wind speed

(D) Directly proportional to the radius of the blades of the windmill

25. Which of the following statement is correct?

(A) Tidal energy is a renewable source of energy

(B) Tidal energy becomes unavailable during dry spell for many years

(C) Tidal power plant requires large area of valuable land

(D) There are very few suitable sites available for construction of dams

26. Acid rain happens because __________.

(A) Sun leads to heating of upper layer of atmosphere

(B) Electrical charges are produced due to friction amongst clouds

(C) Burning of fossil fuels release oxides of carbon, nitrogen and sulphur in the atmosphere

(D) Earth's atmosphere contains acids

27. In a hydro power plant __________.

(A) Potential energy possessed by stored water is converted into electricity

(B) Kinetic energy possessed by stored water is converted into electricity

(C) Electricity is extracted from chemical reactions in water

(D) Water is converted into steam to generate electricity

28. Which of the following is the ultimate source of energy ?

(A) Water

(B) Fossil fuel

(C) Sun

(D) Air

29. Ocean thermal energy (OTE) is due to __________.

(A) Energy stored by waves in the ocean

(B) Temperature difference at different levels in the ocean

(C) Pressure difference at different levels in the ocean

(D) Tides arising out in the ocean

30. Which part of the solar cooker is responsible for greenhouse effect?

(A) Glass sheet

(B) Mirror

(C) Outer cover of the solar cooker

(D) Coating with black colour inside the box

## HOTS (ACHIEVERS SECTION)

31. The electricity generated by a windmill depends on __________.

(A) Height of the tower

(B) Velocity of wind

(C) Size of the blades

(D) All of these

32. Choose the false statement __________.

(A) Wave power output is of variable nature

(B) Wave energy is renewable and pollution free

(C) Wave power is inexpensive to explore

(D) Wave power is same as wave energy

33. A major problem in harnessing nuclear energy through nuclear fission is __________.

(A) splitting the nuclear

(B) disposal of nuclear wastes

(C) converting nuclear energy to electric energy

(D) sustaining chain reaction

34. In a hydro power plant,
    (A) potential energy possessed by stored water is converted into electricity.
    (B) kinetic energy possessed by stored water is converted into potential energy
    (C) electricity is extracted from water
    (D) water is converted into steam to produce electricity.

35. Acid rain occurs because ___________.
    (A) the earth's atmosphere contains acids.
    (B) electrical charges are produced due to friction amongst clouds.
    (C) The sun leads to heating of upper layer of atmosphere.
    (D) burning of fossil fuels releases oxides of carbon, nitrogen and sulphur in the atmosphere.

| | | | | | | | | | | | | | | | | | | | |
|---|---|---|---|---|---|---|---|---|---|---|---|---|---|---|---|---|---|---|---|
| 1. | Ⓐ Ⓑ Ⓒ Ⓓ | 8. | Ⓐ Ⓑ Ⓒ Ⓓ | 15. | Ⓐ Ⓑ Ⓒ Ⓓ | 22 | Ⓐ Ⓑ Ⓒ Ⓓ | 29. | Ⓐ Ⓑ Ⓒ Ⓓ |
| 2. | Ⓐ Ⓑ Ⓒ Ⓓ | 9. | Ⓐ Ⓑ Ⓒ Ⓓ | 16. | Ⓐ Ⓑ Ⓒ Ⓓ | 23. | Ⓐ Ⓑ Ⓒ Ⓓ | 30. | Ⓐ Ⓑ Ⓒ Ⓓ |
| 3. | Ⓐ Ⓑ Ⓒ Ⓓ | 10. | Ⓐ Ⓑ Ⓒ Ⓓ | 17. | Ⓐ Ⓑ Ⓒ Ⓓ | 24. | Ⓐ Ⓑ Ⓒ Ⓓ | 31. | Ⓐ Ⓑ Ⓒ Ⓓ |
| 4. | Ⓐ Ⓑ Ⓒ Ⓓ | 11. | Ⓐ Ⓑ Ⓒ Ⓓ | 18. | Ⓐ Ⓑ Ⓒ Ⓓ | 25. | Ⓐ Ⓑ Ⓒ Ⓓ | 32. | Ⓐ Ⓑ Ⓒ Ⓓ |
| 5. | Ⓐ Ⓑ Ⓒ Ⓓ | 12. | Ⓐ Ⓑ Ⓒ Ⓓ | 19. | Ⓐ Ⓑ Ⓒ Ⓓ | 26. | Ⓐ Ⓑ Ⓒ Ⓓ | 33. | Ⓐ Ⓑ Ⓒ Ⓓ |
| 6. | Ⓐ Ⓑ Ⓒ Ⓓ | 13. | Ⓐ Ⓑ Ⓒ Ⓓ | 20. | Ⓐ Ⓑ Ⓒ Ⓓ | 27. | Ⓐ Ⓑ Ⓒ Ⓓ | 34. | Ⓐ Ⓑ Ⓒ Ⓓ |
| 7. | Ⓐ Ⓑ Ⓒ Ⓓ | 14. | Ⓐ Ⓑ Ⓒ Ⓓ | 21. | Ⓐ Ⓑ Ⓒ Ⓓ | 28. | Ⓐ Ⓑ Ⓒ Ⓓ | 35. | Ⓐ Ⓑ Ⓒ Ⓓ |

# OUR ENVIRONMENT

## LEARNING OBJECTIVES

➤ Ecosystem and its components
➤ Trophic levels of a food chain
➤ Garbage disposal in daily routine
➤ The food chain
➤ Ozone depletion and its effects

## MULTIPLE CHOICE QUESTIONS

1. Which one of the following is not a terrestrial ecosystem?
   (A) Desert
   (B) Grass land
   (C) Forest
   (D) River

2. What will happen if deer is missing in the food chain given below:

   Grass → Deer → Tiger

   (A) The population of grass decreases as more deer are saved
   (B) The population of tigers increases as they can eat more grass
   (C) The population of tigers decreases and the grass increases enormously
   (D) None of these

3. The one which is not biodegradable material is ____________.
   (A) Cotton
   (B) Animal bone
   (C) Aluminium foil
   (D) Wooden chair

4. Which of the following is not a producer?
   (A) Zooplankton
   (B) Grass
   (C) Phytoplankton
   (D) Paddy

5. One of the following is a micro-consumer. This one is ____________.
   (A) Ant
   (B) Lice
   (C) Mosquito
   (D) Fungi

6. Organisms which synthesize carbohydrates from inorganic compounds by using radiant energy are called ____________.
   (A) Decomposers
   (B) Herbivores
   (C) Producers
   (D) Omnivores

7. Organism of a higher trophic level which feed on several types of organisms belonging to the number of lower trophic levels of different food chains constitute the ____________.
   (A) Ecosystem
   (B) Food web
   (C) Ecological pyramid
   (D) Food network

8. Which one of these is a non-biodegradable waste?
   (A) Polythene
   (B) PVC
   (C) Bakellite
   (D) All of these

9. Some organisms produce their own food using simple inorganic substances under photosynthesis process. Identify the organism which does this activity?
   (A) Green Algae
   (B) Fungi
   (C) Bacteria
   (D) Virus

10. Which one among the following is a lotic ecosystem?
    (A) River
    (B) Stream
    (C) Spring
    (D) All of these

11. Which of these is a lentic ecosystem?
    (A) Lake
    (B) Pond
    (C) Swamp
    (D) All of these

12. Which of these is a terrestrial ecosystem?
    (A) Desert
    (B) Forest
    (C) Grassland
    (D) All of these

13. The use of _____________ will pollute the environment.
    (A) Carry bag made of nylon cloth
    (B) Carry bag made of cotton cloth
    (C) Carry bag made of jute fibre
    (D) Carry bag made of paper

14. Which of the following act as decomposers in an ecosystem?
    (A) Cyanobacteria
    (B) Lactobacillus bacteria
    (C) Putrefying bacteria
    (D) Rhizobium bacteria

15. In the food chain comprising of a snake, grass, insect and frog, the secondary consumer is _____________.
    (A) Snake
    (B) Frog
    (C) Insect
    (D) Grass

16. If 10 Joules of energy is available of producer level, then the energy transferred to the lion in the following food chain is _____________.

    Plants → Deer → Lion

    (A) 1 J             (B) 5 J
    (C) 0.1 J           (D) 0.5 J

17. The ozone layer is composed of _____________.
    (A) O
    (B) $O_3$
    (C) $O_2$
    (D) Combination of 3 oxygen atoms

18. The Sahara desert was formed over a period of time due to _____________.
    (A) Excessive deforestation
    (B) Excessive killing of large herbivores
    (C) Excessive killing of large carnivores
    (D) Excessive use of poisonous chemicals

19. The ultimate source of energy in our ecosystem is _____________.
    (A) Water
    (B) Sun
    (C) Air
    (D) Microbes

20. The 'Ten-percent Law' of energy flow in food chain is proposed by _____________.
    (A) Raymond Lindeman
    (B) Charles Lindeman
    (C) Raymond Hilary
    (D) Lindeman Jhones

21. What provides the energy which then flows through a food chain?
    (A) Glucose
    (B) Oxygen
    (C) Respiration
    (D) Sunlight

22. In a food chain the energy available for transfer at different trophic levels is the form of _____________.
    (A) Heat energy
    (B) Light energy
    (C) Mechanical energy
    (D) Chemical energy

23. The flow of energy in an ecosystem is always _____________.
    (A) Cyclic
    (B) Unidirectional

(C) Multidirectional

(D) Bidirectional

24. In the food chain given below, if the energy at fourth trophic level is 3 kJ, what was the energy available at producer level?

(A) 30 kJ

(B) 300 kJ

(C) 3000 kJ

(D) 3 kJ

25. The excessive exposure of humans to ultraviolet rays results in ——————.

(A) Damage to immune system

(B) Skin cancer

(C) Both (A) and (B)

(D) Neither (A) nor (B)

26. Which of the following gets the minimum energy through the food chain in an ecosystem?

(A) Herbivores

(B) Producers

(C) Carnivores

(D) Large carnivores

27. Most of the water surface of a lake is covered with algae. This algae is part of the food chain which also includes small fish, bird, larvae and a big fish. Which of the following will obtain maximum energy?

(A) Larvae

(B) Small fish

(C) Bird

(D) Big fish

28. Oxygen molecule $(O_2)$ is converted into ozone $(O_3)$ by the action of ——————.

(A) Infrared radiations

(B) Ultraviolet radiations

(C) Gamma radiations

(D) Cosmic radiations

29. Which of the following is the source of CFC gas, released into the atmosphere causing ozone depletion?

(A) Coolers

(B) Refrigerators

(C) Vehicles

(D) Factory

30. Which of the following cannot be added in a composting pit to prepare compost?

(A) Sunflower plants

(B) Fruit and vegetable peels

(C) Plastic flowers

(D) Red earth worms

## HOTS (ACHIEVERS SECTION)

31. The 10% of energy available to be transferred from one trophic level to another is in the form of —————— energy.

(A) chemical

(B) solar

(C) light

(D) mechanical

32. The main reason for the abundant coliform bacteria in the water of River Ganga is ——————.

(A) immersion of ashes of the dead body into the river.

(B) washing of clothes on the banks of the river.

(C) discharge of industrial wastes into the river.

(D) disposal of unburnt corpses into river water.

33. The gas ———————— was not present in early atmosphere of the earth?

(A) Methane

(B) Ammonia

(C) Hydrogen sulphide

(D) Oxygen

34. Which of the following is not true.
   (A) The earth receives an average of 4 KWh/m² solar energy daily.
   (B) A thermal power plant generates only heat energy by burning fossil fuels like coal.
   (C) Ocean thermal energy is the solar energy stored in the sea water.
   (D) None of these

35. Ozone forms by the combination of free oxygen atoms and oxygen molecules. How do free oxygen atoms form at higher levels of the atmosphere?

   (A) By splitting molecular oxygen into free oxygen atoms in the presence of low-energy UV radiations.
   (B) By splitting molecular oxygen into free oxygen atoms in the presence of high-energy UV radiations.
   (C) By the combination of two molecular oxygen in the presence of high energy UV radiations.
   (D) By the combination of two free oxygen atoms in the presence of lower energy UV radiations.

# LOGICAL REASONING

15



- ➤ Different types of analogy
- ➤ Different types of classification and related questions
- ➤ Concept of Coding and Decoding
- ➤ Concept of Time sequence test
- ➤ Different directions and their usage
- ➤ Alphabet Test concepts
- ➤ Different types of blood relation
- ➤ Problems based on mathematical operations
- ➤ Series questions based on figures
- ➤ Concept of Paper folding and related questions
- ➤ Concept of Paper cutting and related questions
- ➤ Mirror image of letters

## MULTIPLE CHOICE QUESTIONS

1. 2836 : 13; 9423 : 14; 7229 : ?
   - (A) 20
   - (B) 18
   - (C) 16
   - (D) 12

2. 211 : 333 :: 356 : ?
   - (A) 358
   - (B) 388
   - (C) 423
   - (D) 459

3. TSR : FED :: WVU : ?
   - (A) MLK
   - (B) GFH
   - (C) CAB
   - (D) PQS

4. (A) Snake
   - (B) Whale
   - (C) Lizard
   - (D) Crocodile

5. (A) Bangle
   - (B) Necklace
   - (C) Ring
   - (D) Ornament

6. (A) Canada
   - (B) Europe
   - (C) Australia
   - (D) Asia

7. If COME is coded as BNLD, then BRING will be coded as ____________.
   - (A) BSHMF
   - (B) BPJMH
   - (C) AQHMF
   - (D) APJMH

8. In a certain code if SILVER is REVLIS, then BLACK will be coded as ____________.
   - (A) KCALB
   - (B) KACBL
   - (C) KCLAB
   - (D) KCBAL

9. In a certain code 3456 is coded as ROPE, 15526 is coded as APPLE. then 54613 will be coded as ____________.
   - (A) PEORA
   - (B) RPOEA
   - (C) PROEA
   - (D) POEAR

10. If the seventh day of a month is three days earlier than Friday. What day will it be on the nineteenth day of the month?
    - (A) Friday
    - (B) Sunday
    - (C) Monday
    - (D) Wednesday

11. In a queue P is eighteenth from the front while $Q$ is sixteenth from the back. If $R$ is twenty fourth from the front and is exactly in the middle position of $P$ and $Q$, then how many persons are there in queue?
    - (A) 47
    - (B) 46
    - (C) 45
    - (D) 48

12. If 3 is subtracted from the middle digit of each of the following numbers and then the positions of the digits are reversed. Which of the following will be the last digit of the middle number after they are arranged in descending order
    589, 362, 554, 371, 442

(A) 1                    (B) 2
(C) 3                    (D) 4

13. John leaves his house and walks 12 km towards North. He turns right and walks another 12 km. He turns right again and walks 12 km more and turns left to walk 5 km. How far is he from his home and in which direction?
(A) 7 km, East         (B) 24 km, East
(C) 10 km, East       (D) 17 km, East

14. $A$, $B$, $C$, $D$, $E$, $F$, $G$, and $H$ are sitting around a round table in the same order for group discussion at equal distance. Their positions are clockwise. If $G$ sits in the North, then what will be the position of $D$.
(A) South-east        (B) South
(C) South-west       (D) East

15. Dinesh starts walking straight towards east. After walking 75 meters, he turns to the left and walks 25 meters straight. Again he turns to the left walks a distance of 40 meters straight, again he turns to the left and walks a distance of 25 meters. How far is he from the starting point?
(A) 50 meters          (B) 25 meteres
(C) 35 meters          (D) 115 meters

16. UNCONSCIOUS
(A) NOSE              (B) COIN
(C) SUN                (D) SON

17. CONTEMPORARY
(A) PARROT
(B) PRAYER
(C) COMPANY
(D) CARPENTER

18. REFRIGERATE
(A) REFER            (B) REGENERATE
(C) MANTLE        (D) DENTAL

19. Soni who is Mishra's daughter says to Punam, "your mother Mamta is the youngest sister of my father. Mishra's father's child is Prabhat". How is Prabhat related to Punam?
(A) Father             (B) Uncle
(C) Father in law     (D) Grandmother

20. Pointing towards a man in the photograph Rekha said, "He is the son of only son of my grandmother." How is man related to Rekha?
(A) Cousin            (B) Son
(C) Nephew         (D) Brother

21. Ramesh told Suresh, "Yesterday I defeated the only brother of the daughter of my grandmother". Whom did Ramesh defeat?
(A) Father            (B) Son
(C) Brother         (D) Father in law

22. If 20 - 10 means 200, 8 ÷ 4 means 12, 6 × 2 means 4, then 100 - 10 × 1000 ÷ 1000 + 100 × 10 = ?
(A) 20               (B) 1000
(C) 0                (D) 1900

23. If $A$ stands for +, $B$ stands for -, $C$ stands for × then what is the value of $(10\,C\,4)\,A\,(4\,C\,4)\,B\,6$?
(A) 56               (B) 46
(C) 60               (D) 50

24. If + means -, - means ×, ÷ means + and × means ÷, then $(3 - 5 ÷ 19) × 8 + 6 = ?$
(A) 2                (B) 4
(C) 8                (D) -1

<table>
<tr><th>PROBLEM FIGURES</th><th>ANSWER FIGURES</th></tr>
</table>

25. 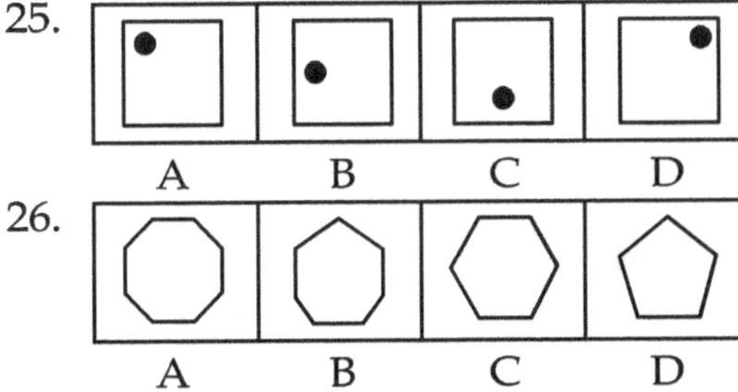

26.

  A       B       C       D        (A)    (B)    (C)    (D)    (e)

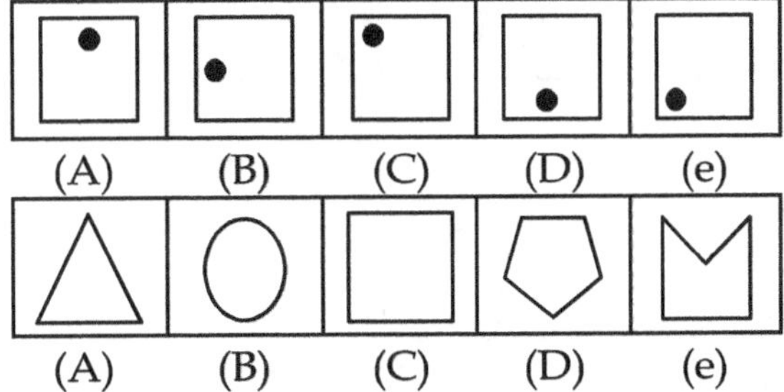

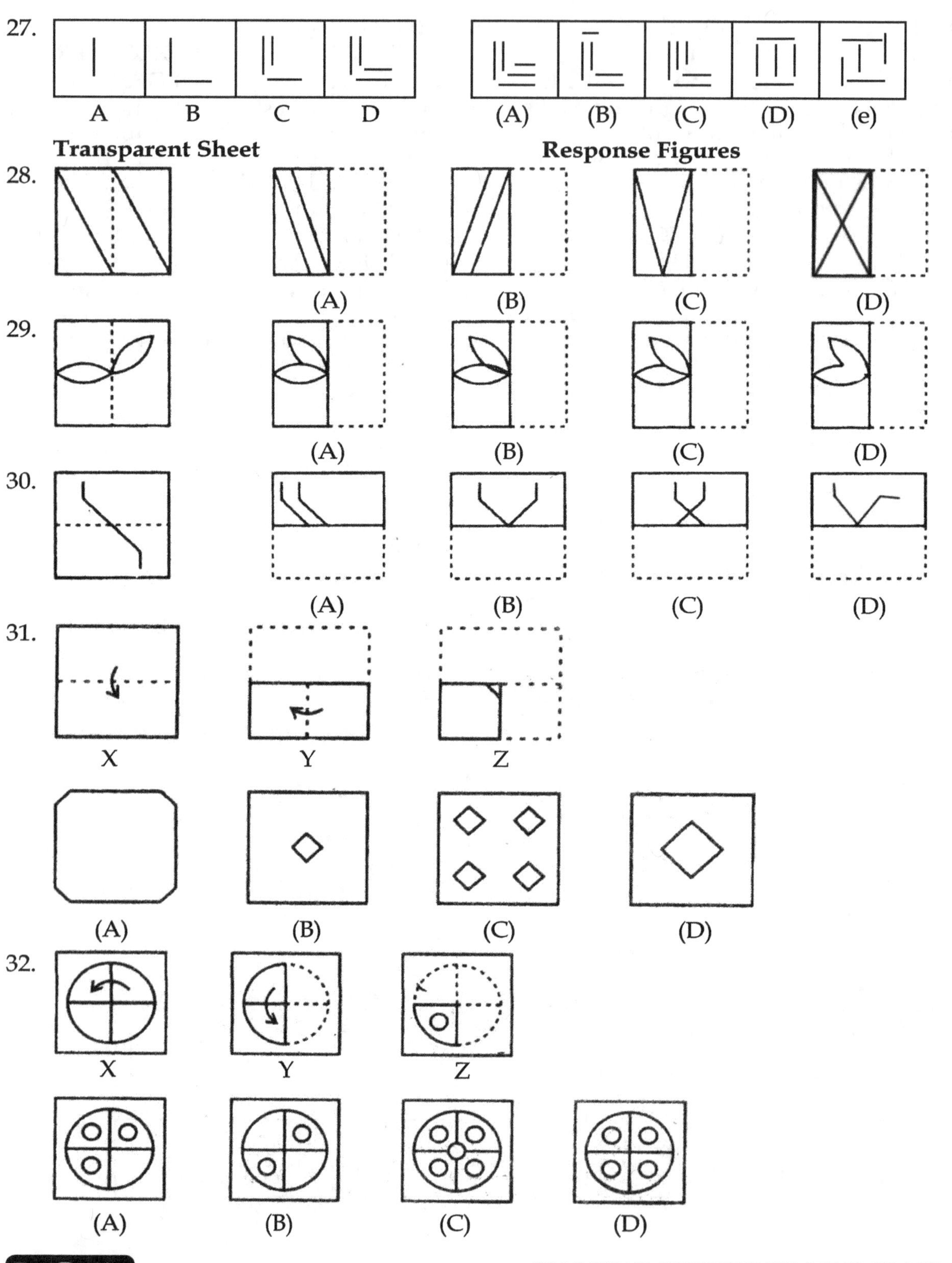

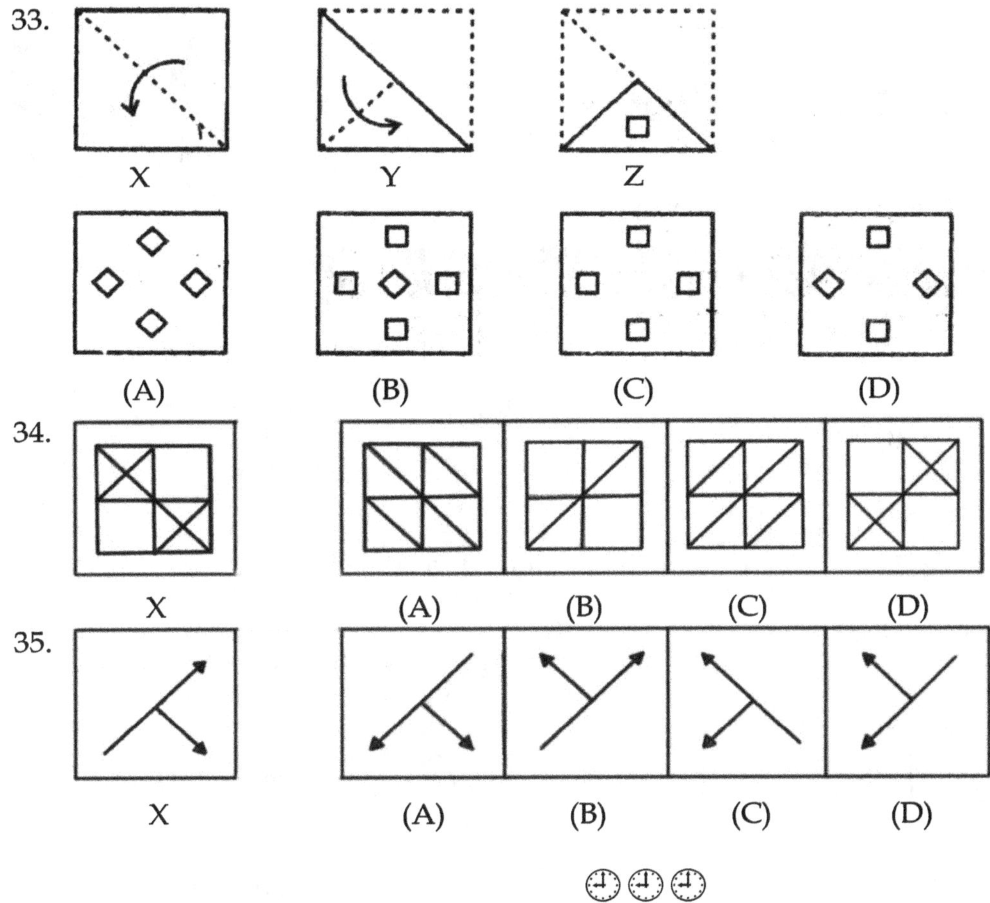

33. X    Y    Z

(A)    (B)    (C)    (D)

34. X    (A)    (B)    (C)    (D)

35. X    (A)    (B)    (C)    (D)



| 1. | Ⓐ Ⓑ Ⓒ Ⓓ | 8. | Ⓐ Ⓑ Ⓒ Ⓓ | 15. | Ⓐ Ⓑ Ⓒ Ⓓ | 22. | Ⓐ Ⓑ Ⓒ Ⓓ | 29. | Ⓐ Ⓑ Ⓒ Ⓓ |
|---|---|---|---|---|---|---|---|---|---|
| 2. | Ⓐ Ⓑ Ⓒ Ⓓ | 9. | Ⓐ Ⓑ Ⓒ Ⓓ | 16. | Ⓐ Ⓑ Ⓒ Ⓓ | 23. | Ⓐ Ⓑ Ⓒ Ⓓ | 30. | Ⓐ Ⓑ Ⓒ Ⓓ |
| 3. | Ⓐ Ⓑ Ⓒ Ⓓ | 10. | Ⓐ Ⓑ Ⓒ Ⓓ | 17. | Ⓐ Ⓑ Ⓒ Ⓓ | 24. | Ⓐ Ⓑ Ⓒ Ⓓ | 31. | Ⓐ Ⓑ Ⓒ Ⓓ |
| 4. | Ⓐ Ⓑ Ⓒ Ⓓ | 11. | Ⓐ Ⓑ Ⓒ Ⓓ | 18. | Ⓐ Ⓑ Ⓒ Ⓓ | 25. | Ⓐ Ⓑ Ⓒ Ⓓ | 32. | Ⓐ Ⓑ Ⓒ Ⓓ |
| 5. | Ⓐ Ⓑ Ⓒ Ⓓ | 12. | Ⓐ Ⓑ Ⓒ Ⓓ | 19. | Ⓐ Ⓑ Ⓒ Ⓓ | 26. | Ⓐ Ⓑ Ⓒ Ⓓ | 33. | Ⓐ Ⓑ Ⓒ Ⓓ |
| 6. | Ⓐ Ⓑ Ⓒ Ⓓ | 13. | Ⓐ Ⓑ Ⓒ Ⓓ | 20. | Ⓐ Ⓑ Ⓒ Ⓓ | 27. | Ⓐ Ⓑ Ⓒ Ⓓ | 34. | Ⓐ Ⓑ Ⓒ Ⓓ |
| 7. | Ⓐ Ⓑ Ⓒ Ⓓ | 14. | Ⓐ Ⓑ Ⓒ Ⓓ | 21. | Ⓐ Ⓑ Ⓒ Ⓓ | 28. | Ⓐ Ⓑ Ⓒ Ⓓ | 35. | Ⓐ Ⓑ Ⓒ Ⓓ |

# MODEL TEST PAPER

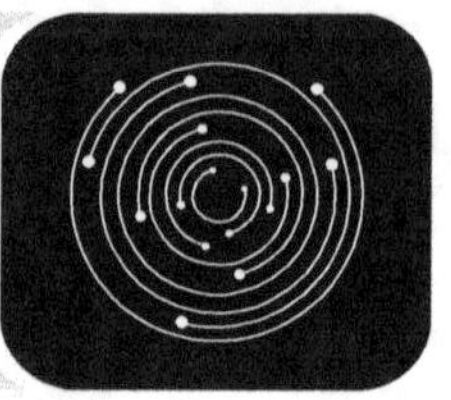

## MULTIPLE CHOICE QUESTIONS

1. Find the missing term in the following series.
   10, 37, 101, 226, ?
   (A) 432      (B) 442
   (C) 369      (D) 378

2. In a certain code language, EMPTY is coded as FOSXD. How will STRING be coded in that language?
   (A) TVUSMS      (B) TUVMSM
   (C) TVUMSM      (D) TUVMMS

3. Complete the following analogy.
   EFRT : GJXB : : DNSL : ?
   (A) FRYT      (B) GRYT
   (C) FSYT      (D) FRZT

4. Which number should come next in the given series?
   600, 650, 702, 756, ?
   (A) 760      (B) 789
   (C) 812      (D) 841

5. Which of the following atoms contains only one proton and one neutron in the nucleus?
   (A) Tritium      (B) Protium
   (C) Deuterium      (D) Helium

6. For general consideration:
   In an acidic solution: $[H_3O^+] > [OH^-]$ and the pH < 7.
   In a basic medium: $[H_3O^+] < [OH^-]$ and pH > 7.
   Which of the following statements about pH and $H^+$ ion concentration is incorrect?
   (A) Addition of one drop of concentrated HCl in $NH_4OH$ solution decreases pH of the solution.
   (B) A solution of a mixture of one equivalent of each of $CH_3COOH$ and NaOH has a pH of 7.
   (C) pH of pure neutral water at 25°C is 7.
   (D) A cold and concentrated $H_2SO_4$ has lower $H^+$ ion concentration than a dilute solution of $H_2SO_4$.

7. The bases which dissociate in their aqueous solution to produce one hydroxyl ion per molecule of the base are referred to as
   (A) triacidic      (B) diacidic
   (C) monoacidic      (D) None of these

8. Which of the following methods can be used to separate $NH_4Cl$ from NaCl?
   Which figure given below shows the CD after it rotated (turned) 90° clockwise?
   (A) Heating the solid mixture in a test tube
   (B) Dissolving the mixture in $CS_2$
   (C) Moving a magnet through the mixture
   (D) Passing the mixture through a sieve

9. Which of the following is a non-commercial conventional source of energy?
   (A) Coal      (B) Petroleum
   (C) Firewood      (D) Electricity

10. Which of the following chemical equations represents precipitation reaction?
    (A) $HCl (aq) + NaOH (aq) \rightarrow NaCl (aq) + H_2O (g)$
    (B) $2KI + PbSO_4 \rightarrow PbI_2 + K_2SO$
    (C) $2H_2 (g) + O_2 (g) \rightarrow 2 H_2O (g)$
    (D) $2H_2 (g) + O_2 (g) \rightarrow 2 H_2O (g)$

11. How many species (reactants and products) in the following reaction are in the gaseous state?
    $2Fe + 3H_2O \rightarrow Fe_2O_3 + 3H_2$
    (A) 1      (B) 2
    (C) 3      (D) 4

12. What is the chemical name for Vitamin C?
   (A) Folic Acid          (B) Biotin
   (C) Ascorbic Acid       (D) Tocopherols
13. Which of the following is not a limitation of Mendeleev's periodic table?
   (A) Position of the noble gases
   (B) Position of isotopes
   (C) Position of hydrogen
   (D) Anomalous pairs
14. What is the scattering of light by the particles in a colloidal solution called?
   (A) Tyndall effect
   (B) Rayleigh scattering change
   (C) Pure spectrum
   (D) Angular dispersion
15. Which of the following elements belongs to the group IA in the modern periodic table?
   (A) Be          (B) Rb
   (C) He          (D) B
16. Which of the following can be defined as the feeding of complex organic matter by ingestion, which is subsequently digested and absorbed?
   (A) Holozoic nutrition
   (B) Parasitic nutrition
   (C) Chemosynthesis nutrition
   (D) Saprotrophic nutrition
17. Phagocytosis is the ingestion of bacteria or other material by phagocytes and amoeboid protozoans. High abundance of which of the following organelles in their cytosol will help in the process?
   (A) Golgi bodies
   (B) Endoplasmic reticulum
   (C) Mitochondria
   (D) Lysosome
18. In some organisms, the unfertilised egg can develop into a new individual. What is this development without fertilisation called?
   (A) Totipotency       (B) Emasculation
   (C) Parthenogenesis   (D) Hybridisation
19. The hormone that promotes secondary sexual characters in human male is:
   (A) Oestrogen
   (B) Progesterone
   (C) Luteinising hormone
   (D) Testosterone
20. In some animals, extreme environmental conditions determine the sex of the child. In turtles, males are predominant below: $24748 - ? + 4239 \times 3 = 33918$
   (A) 35°C              (B) 27°C
   (C) 25°C              (D) 39°C
21. Germ cells consist of only a single set of genes. These are produced by the process of
   (A) meiosis
   (B) mitosis
   (C) binary fission
   (D) parthenogenesis
22. Which property makes $CO_2$ an effective heat-trapping greenhouse gas?
   (A) Ability to absorb and re-emit infrared radiation
   (B) Ability to emit ultraviolet radiation
   (C) Ability to absorb cosmic rays
   (D) Ability to release gamma rays and heat
23. The genetic material of endangered species can be preserved by
   (A) gene pool
   (B) gene library
   (C) gene bank
   (D) gene laboratory
24. What is the full form of OTEC with context to energy?
   (A) Ocean Thermal Energy Conversion
   (B) Ocean Thermal Energy Consumption
   (C) Over Thermal Energy Consumption
   (D) Ocean Temperature Energy Conversion
25. What is a biodiversity hotspot?
   (A) Region having volcano eruptions
   (B) Region where rocks melt to generate magma
   (C) Biogeographic region with a significant reservoir of biodiversity that is under threat from humans
   (D) Biogeographic region with a significant reservoir of biodiversity that has extreme weather condition

26. What is the pigmented vascular layer of the eyeball between the retina and the sclera called?
(A) Iris (B) Choroid
(C) Cornea (D) Pupil

27. An object is moving towards the plane mirror with speed 'v'. Then, the speed of the image as observed by an object is
(A) 2v
(B) v
(C) 4v
(D) Cannot be determined

28. Which of the following is used to reverse the direction of current in a DC motor?
(A) Solenoid
(B) Switch
(C) Commutator
(D) Magnetic needle

29. Which of the following materials can be used to increase the intensity of the magnetic field in an electromagnet?
(A) Aluminium (B) Soft iron core
(C) Wood (D) Plastic

30. The solar energy reaching the periphery of the Earth's atmosphere is considered to be constant for all practical purposes, and is known as the solar constant. What is its value?
(A) $1.14$ kJ m$^{-2}$ (B) $1.2$ kJ m$^{-2}$
(C) $1.4$ kJ m$^{-2}$ (D) $1.44$ kJ m$^{-2}$

31. Which among the following statements are true about slaking of lime and the solution formed?
(I) It is an exothermic reaction.
(II) It is an endothermic reaction.
(III) The pH of resulting solution is greater than 7.
(IV) The pH of resulting solution is less than 7.
(A) (I) and (III) (B) (II) and (III)
(C) (I) and (IV) (D) (II) and (IV)

32. The following are given some statements. Select the option which shows the correct statement(s) regarding metals and non-metals.
Statements:
I. Metals have 1 to 3 electrons in the valence shell and non-metals have 4-8 electrons in their valence shell.
II. Metallic oxides give acids on reaction with water and non-metallic oxides give bases on reaction with water.
III. Among the metals, the less electropositive metals displace the more electropositive metals from their salts.
IV. Non-metals lose electrons from their valence shell to attain a stable configuration and form cations.
V. Metals like Au and Pt also form oxides.
(A) Only I (B) Both I and II
(C) I, II and III (D) I, III and V

33. A bar magnet is released into a copper ring which is directly below it. What is true about the acceleration of the magnet?
(A) Greater than 'g'
(B) Equal to 'g'
(C) Less than 'g'
(D) Cannot be determined

34. A highly polluted city will not show the growth of
(A) lichens (B) angiosperms
(C) algae (D) bryophytes

35. The presence of which of the following metals causes the teeth of the children to discolour?
(A) Fluorides (B) Chlorides
(C) Phosphates (D) Nitrates

36. The structure that prevents the acidic contents of the stomach from moving upward into the esophagus is
(A) anal sphincter
(B) cardiac sphincter
(C) precapillary sphincter
(D) pyloric sphincter

37. The primary form of sugar transported from the site of photosynthesis to the rest of the plant is
(A) glucose (B) starch
(C) sucrose (D) fructose

38. The pathway which is common to both aerobic and anaerobic pathways of respiration is
(A) glycolysis
(B) Kreb's cycle
(C) electron transport chain
(D) oxidative phosphorylation

39. Match the below mentioned parts of human heart in column I with their appropriate functions in column II.

Column I

(A) Septum
(B) Pulmonary artery
(C) Inferior vena cava
(D) Left auricle

Column II

(i) Carry the deoxygenated blood to right atrium of the heart
(ii) Receives blood from lungs
(iii) Maintains rigidity and support to the heart
(iv) Transports oxygen-depleted blood to lungs

(A) a - iii, b - iv, c - ii, d - i
(B) a - iv, b - iii, c - i, d - ii
(C) a - iii, b - iv, c - i, d - ii
(D) a - iv, b - iii, c - ii, d - i

40. Urea, the principal nitrogenous excretory compound in humans, is synthesised

(A) in the liver but eliminated mostly through kidneys
(B) in kidneys but eliminated mostly through liver
(C) as well as eliminated by kidneys
(D) in liver and also eliminated by the same through bile

41. Rohan was bitten by a malaria-infected mosquito that led to the release of malarial parasites into his blood. The main target organ where these parasites reproduce will be:

(A) Spleen
(B) Liver
(C) Kidney
(D) Small intestine

42. Snigdha's grandmother suffered from a leg fracture. The doctor told her that her grandmother had a very low calcium level. Along with that she also had vitamin deficiency that helps in absorption of calcium in the body. The vitamin is:

(A) Vitamin C
(B) Vitamin D
(C) Vitamin E
(D) Vitamin A

43. It is not advised to store curd and other sour substances in copper or brass vessels because

(A) Curd and sour substances contain acids
(B) Curd and sour substances contain bases which are bitter
(C) Curd and sour substances lose their flavour and freshness if preserved in metal containers
(D) Curd and sour substances rot if preserved in metal containers

44. Which of the following statements is/are the correct reason(s) for rubbing a magnesium ribbon with sand paper before burning it in air?

I. The surface is covered with a layer of magnesium oxide.

II. Cleaning gives a better reaction as magnesium is a moderately reactive metal.

(A) Only I
(B) Only II
(C) Both I and II
(D) Both I and II are false.

45. The position of an element in the periodic table is related to its electronic configuration. In this context, identify the correct statement among the following.

(A) Elements across a period show a decrease in the number of valence electrons.
(B) Atoms with similar electronic configuration are placed in the same group.
(C) The number of valence electrons is not the same for every element in the group.
(D) None of these

46. Gibberellins were discovered by a Japanese botanist while studying the "foolish seedling" disease in rice. They were first isolated from the fungus known as
(A) Gibberella moniliformis
(B) Gibberella fujikuroi
(C) Gibberella acuminata
(D) Gibberella africana

47. It is a biological fact that human stomach produces acid. Which of the following is not a role of hydrochloric acid produced by the stomach?
(A) Sterilisation of the food
(B) Prevention of harmful bacteria from entering the GI tract
(C) Creation of optimal condition that promotes bacterial growth
(D) Activation of pepsinogen to pepsin

48. Villi are adapted for the maximum absorption of digested food molecules. Which property makes them suitable for the same?
(A) The folded villi greatly increase the surface area of the intestine.
(B) The villi are made of a single layer of thin cells.
(C) Beneath the villi is an extensive blood capillary network.
(D) All of these

49. Site of transfer of oxygen and other nutrients from the bloodstream to other tissues in the body is
(A) capillaries
(B) veins
(C) arteries
(D) bronchioles

50. "These are very beneficial for an organism while reproducing. These are distributed easily by air to far-off places to avoid competition at one place. Large numbers are produced in a single sporangium and they are also covered with thick walls to avoid dehydration." From the passage of the arguments given above, find out the unit of reproduction being discussed.
(A) Spore
(B) Pollen
(C) Reduction body
(D) Gemmule

| | | | | | | | | | | | | | | | | | | | | | | | |
|---|---|---|---|---|---|---|---|---|---|---|---|---|---|---|---|---|---|---|---|---|---|---|---|---|
| 1. | A | B | C | D | 11. | A | B | C | D | 21. | A | B | C | D | 31. | A | B | C | D | 41. | A | B | C | D |
| 2. | A | B | C | D | 12. | A | B | C | D | 22. | A | B | C | D | 32. | A | B | C | D | 42. | A | B | C | D |
| 3. | A | B | C | D | 13. | A | B | C | D | 23. | A | B | C | D | 33. | A | B | C | D | 43. | A | B | C | D |
| 4. | A | B | C | D | 14. | A | B | C | D | 24. | A | B | C | D | 34. | A | B | C | D | 44. | A | B | C | D |
| 5. | A | B | C | D | 15. | A | B | C | D | 25. | A | B | C | D | 35. | A | B | C | D | 45. | A | B | C | D |
| 6. | A | B | C | D | 16. | A | B | C | D | 26. | A | B | C | D | 36. | A | B | C | D | 46. | A | B | C | D |
| 7. | A | B | C | D | 17. | A | B | C | D | 27. | A | B | C | D | 37. | A | B | C | D | 47. | A | B | C | D |
| 8. | A | B | C | D | 18. | A | B | C | D | 28. | A | B | C | D | 38. | A | B | C | D | 48. | A | B | C | D |
| 9. | A | B | C | D | 19. | A | B | C | D | 29. | A | B | C | D | 39. | A | B | C | D | 49. | A | B | C | D |
| 10. | A | B | C | D | 20. | A | B | C | D | 30. | A | B | C | D | 40. | A | B | C | D | 50. | A | B | C | D |

# HINTS AND SOLUTIONS

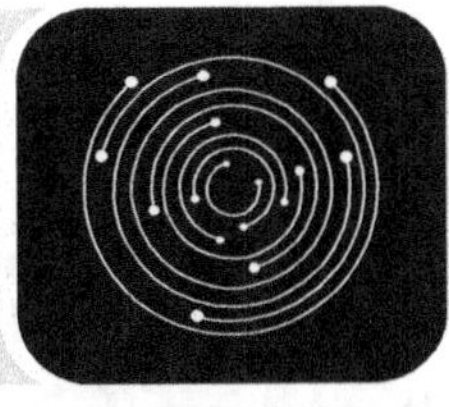

## 1. CHEMICAL REACTIONS AND EQUATIONS

### Answer Key

| 1. (B) | 2. (C) | 3. (B) | 4. (D) | 5. (D) | 6. (D) | 7. (D) | 8. (B) | 9. (C) | 10. (C) |
|---|---|---|---|---|---|---|---|---|---|
| 11. (C) | 12. (A) | 13. (A) | 14. (C) | 15. (A) | 16. (B) | 17. (B) | 18. (B) | 19. (C) | 20. (A) |
| 21. (C) | 22. (D) | 23. (C) | 24. (A) | 25. (C) | | | | | |

**3.** (B)

$$2 H_2O\,(l) \xrightarrow{\text{Electrolysis}} 2H_{2(g)} + O_{2(g)}$$

Mole ratio of $H_2$ to $O_2$ liberated $= 2 : 1$.

**5.** (D)

Galvanisation is the process of coating iron with zinc in order to prevent its rusting.

**6.** (D)

Nitrogen and Helium are inert gases and prevent the oxidation of oil and hence they prevent the rancidity.

**14.** (C)

Only reaction (ii) is a double displacement reaction because cations/anions of both the salts are exchanged.

**21.** (C)

At the reaction temperature, $H_2$ gas combine with $O_2$ gas to form $H_2O$ vapour.

### HOTS (ACHIEVERS SECTION)

| 26. (D) | 27. (A) | 28. (A) | 29. (D) | 30. (B) |
|---|---|---|---|---|

## 2. ACIDS, BASES AND SALTS

### Answer Key

| 1. (C) | 2. (D) | 3. (B) | 4. (A) | 5. (C) | 6. (A) | 7. (C) | 8. (C) | 9. (A) | 10. (C) |
|---|---|---|---|---|---|---|---|---|---|
| 11. (B) | 12. (D) | 13. (B) | 14. (C) | 15. (C) | 16. (C) | 17. (D) | 18. (C) | 19. (A) | 20. (B) |
| 21. (C) | 22. (C) | 23. (C) | 24. (B) | 25. (A) | 26. (C) | 27. (B) | 28. (D) | 29. (C) | 30. (C) |

**1.** (C)

Cupric ions, as they react with excess of ammonia solution to form $[Cu(NH_3)_4]^{2+}$

**3.** (B)

$$pH = - \log [H^+]$$
$$pH = - \log (1 \times 10^{-3}] = - (-3) \log 10$$
$$pH = 3$$

**4.** (A)

Molar concentration of HCl acid solution

$$= \frac{0.02}{2L} = 0.01 \text{ mol L}^{-1}$$
$$= 10^{-2} \text{ mol L}^{-1}$$
$$pH = - \log [H^+]$$
$$pH = - \log (10^{-2})$$

$$pH = 2 \log 10$$
$$pH = 2$$

9. **(A)**

   Line (CaO) reacts with HCl acid to form $CaCl_2$ and $H_2O.NOCO_2$ is produced.

10. **(C)**

    Citric acid is not a mineral acid but an organic acid present in citrus fruits.

14. **(C)**

    Some metal oxides (like $Na_2O$, CaO, etc.) react with water to form metal hydroxides (bases) only and not salt and acid.

19. **(C)**

    $C_2H_5OH$ is ethyl alcohol which does not give $OH^-$ ions in the solution.

    Hence, it is not base.

21. **(C)**

    $pH = 4$ means $[H^+] = 10^{-4}$ M. $pH = 10$ means $(H^+) = 10^{-10}$ M or $[H^-] = 10^{-4}$ M

    Thus, one solution is acidic and the other is basic. Further, they have same molarity. On mixing equal volumes, they will neutralize each other completely. The resulting solution will be neutral with $pH = 7.0$

22. **(C)**

    Green vitriol or ferrous sulphate is $FeSO_4.7H_2O$

24. **(B)**

    Glauber's salt is sodium sulphate decahydrate $Na_2SO_4.10H_2O$

28. **(D)**

    Mixing of solution of an acid with the solution of base (neutralization) is exothermic i.e. temperature increases and salt formation takes place.

30. **(C)**

    Turning of the pH paper yellowish – orange shows that the solution is acidic ($pH \approx 5$). To change it to green blue means we want to change it to basic ($pH \approx 8$). This can be done by adding an antacid [like $Mg(OH)_2$]

## 3. METALS AND NON-METALS

### Answer Key

| 1. (C) | 2. (D) | 3. (C) | 4. (B) | 5. (B) | 6. (C) | 7. (B) | 8. (A) | 9. (D) | 10. (B) |
|---|---|---|---|---|---|---|---|---|---|
| 11. (B) | 12. (C) | 13. (C) | 14. (D) | 15. (C) | 16. (A) | 17. (C) | 18. (C) | 19. (C) | 20. (D) |
| 21. (A) | 22. (C) | 23. (B) | 24. (A) | 25. (C) | 26. (B) | 27. (B) | 28. (C) | 29. (D) | 30. (C) |

11. **(B)**

    HCl and $CCl_4$ are covalent compounds.

14. **(D)**

    Fe does not react with cold as well as hot water. It reacts only with steam.

15. **(C)**

    $HNO_3$ is oxidising agent. It oxidzes metal to metal oxide which further dissolves in $HNO_3$ to form metal nitrate and $HNO_3$ itself is reduced to $NO_2$ or NO or $N_2O$ depending upon the nature of the metal and concentration of acid. Mn and Mg are the only metals which react with dilute of $HNO_3$ to produce $H_2$ gas.

16. **(B)**

    Out of the given metals, silver is least reactive and hence will be displaced from its salt solution by other metals.

21. **(A)**

    Being least reactive, gold (Au) and silver (Ag) are found in the native state

23. **(B)**

    $H_2S$ gas of the air attacks silver to form a layer of black $Ag_2S$.

25. **(C)**

    The green coating is due to the formation of basic copper carbonate $CuCO_3$. $Cu(OH)_2$.

| 31. (C) | 32. (A) | 33. (D) | 34. (D) | 35. (C) |
|---|---|---|---|---|

**31. (C)**

Please do not react with conc HCl or conc $HNO_3$ but dissolves in a mixture of conc. HCl and conc. $HNO_3$ in the ratio 3 : 1 called aqua-regia)

**32. (A)**

As X loses electron and Y gains electron to form Z. Hence, Z is an ionic compound.

Ionic compounds have high melting points.

**34. (D)**

Al forms an amphoteric oxide with formula $Al_2O_3$. It can react with acid as well as base.

# 4. CARBON AND ITS COMPOUND

## Answer Key

| 1. (B) | 2. (A) | 3. (A) | 4. (C) | 5. (C) | 6. (B) | 7. (D) | 8. (D) | 9. (C) | 10. (A) |
|---|---|---|---|---|---|---|---|---|---|
| 11. (A) | 12. (B) | 13. (B) | 14. (C) | 15. (D) | 16. (C) | 17. (C) | 18. (C) | 19. (D) | 20. (B) |
| 21. (B) | 22. (A) | 23. (A) | 24. (A) | 25. (B) | 26. (B) | 27. (B) | 28. (C) | 29. (B) | 30. (D) |

**6. (B)**

All the given electorn dot structures are incorrect. The correct electron dot structure is shown below:

$$\ddot{N}\!:\ :\!\ddot{N}$$

**10. (A)**

A molecule of ammonia has only single bond. It has a lone pair of electrons and 3 single bonds.

**12. (B)**

E.C. of Ne = 2, 8

**18. (C)**

Rubbing alcohol is common name of isopropyl alcohol ($C_3H_7OH$)

**19. (D)**

The electron dot structure of water is:

$$H:\ddot{O}:H$$



| 31. (B) | 32. (D) | 33. (C) | 34. (B) | 35. (C) |
|---|---|---|---|---|

# 5. PERIODIC CLASSIFICATION OF ELEMENTS

## Answer Key

| 1. (B) | 2. (B) | 3. (A) | 4. (A) | 5. (D) | 6. (A) | 7. (B) | 8. (D) | 9. (D) | 10. (B) |
|---|---|---|---|---|---|---|---|---|---|
| 11. (B) | 12. (C) | 13. (A) | 14. (D) | 15. (D) | 16. (C) | 17. (B) | 18. (C) | 19. (C) | 20. (C) |
| 21. (B) | 22. (B) | 23. (C) | 24. (B) | 25. (C) | 26. (C) | 27. (C) | 28. (C) | 29. (A) | 30. (B) |

1. **(B)**

Elements in a period have consecutive atomic numbers i.e., 34, 35, 36.

2. **(B)**

2nd period contains elements with atomic numbers 3 (Li), 7 (N) 10 (Ne).

4. **(A)**

Elements which differ in atomic numbers by 8 i.e., 9 (fluorine) and 17 (chlorine).

5. **(D)**

Oxide of Li is basic.

6. **(A)**

Within a period, atomic radii decrease from left to right.

9. **(D)**

Elements with electronic configuration (2, 8) is an inert gas i.e., neon and hence belongs to group 18.

12. **(C)**

The essential constituent of all organic matter is carbon which belongs to group 17.

14. **(D)**

Larger the atomic radius of an element, more easily it can lose its valence electrons. K has the largest atomic radius, therefore it can lose an electron more easily.

15. **(D)**

Elements of 2nd period have smaller size than those of the corresponding elements of the 3rd period. Further in a period, Halogen has the smallest size. Among Na, F, Mg and Al, F has the smallest size and hence it does not lose an electron easily.

17. **(B)**

Eka-aluminium i.e., gallium lies in group III of the Mendeleev's periodic table. Therefore, it has a valency of 3 and forms an oxide having molecular formula $E_2O_3$.

19. **(C)**

Non-metallic character increases from left to right in a period i.e., $Li < Be < C < O < F$.

21. **(B)**

Metallic character increases down a group and decreases along a period. Thus, metallic character increases in the order: Be, Mg, Ca.

24. **(B)**

In a group valency of all elements is fixed because of having the same outer shell electronic configuration while all the remaining three properties increase down the group.

25. **(C)**

Since the element with atomic number 14 i.e., Si forms an acidic oxide and a covalent halide, it must be metalloid.

<table>
<tr><td colspan="5">HOTS (ACHIEVERS SECTION)</td></tr>
<tr><td>31. (D)</td><td>32. (C)</td><td>33. (B)</td><td>34. (C)</td><td>35. (A)</td></tr>
</table>

## 6. LIFE PROCESS

### Answer Key

| 1. (B) | 2. (B) | 3. (A) | 4. (A) | 5. (C) | 6. (D) | 7. (D) | 8. (A) | 9. (A) | 10. (D) |
|---|---|---|---|---|---|---|---|---|---|
| 11. (D) | 12. (B) | 13. (B) | 14. (C) | 15. (B) | 16. (B) | 17. (D) | 18. (B) | 19. (B) | 20. (D) |
| 21. (C) | 22. (D) | 23. (B) | 24. (C) | 25. (B) | 26. (B) | 27. (B) | 28. (A) | 29. (B) | 30. (C) |

<table>
<tr><td colspan="5">HOTS (ACHIEVERS SECTION)</td></tr>
<tr><td>31. (B)</td><td>32. (B)</td><td>33. (B)</td><td>34. (C)</td><td>35. (B)</td></tr>
</table>

### Answer Key

| 1. (B) | 2. (B) | 3. (A) | 4. (A) | 5. (C) | 6. (D) | 7. (D) | 8. (A) | 9. (A) | 10. (D) |
|---|---|---|---|---|---|---|---|---|---|
| 11. (D) | 12. (B) | 13. (B) | 14. (C) | 15. (B) | 16. (B) | 17. (D) | 18. (B) | 19. (B) | 20. (D) |
| 21. (C) | 22. (D) | 23. (B) | 24. (C) | 25. (B) | 26. (B) | 27. (B) | 28. (A) | 29. (B) | 30. (C) |

### HOTS (ACHIEVERS SECTION)

| 31. (D) | 32. (B) | 33. (C) | 34. (A) | 35. (B) |
|---|---|---|---|---|

## 8. HEREDITY AND EVOLUTION

### Answer Key

| 1. (C) | 2. (D) | 3. (A) | 4. (D) | 5. (B) | 6. (C) | 7. (B) | 8. (C) | 9. (B) | 10. (A) |
|---|---|---|---|---|---|---|---|---|---|
| 11. (C) | 12. (B) | 13. (C) | 14. (C) | 15. (B) | 16. (A) | 17. (B) | 18. (D) | 19. (C) | 20. (B) |
| 21. (B) | 22. (B) | 23. (C) | 24. (C) | 25. (B) | 26. (C) | 27. (B) | 28. (C) | 29. (D) | 30. (B) |

### HOTS (ACHIEVERS SECTION)

| 31. (A) | 32. (A) | 33. (B) | 34. (A) | 35. (D) |
|---|---|---|---|---|

## 9. LIGHT

### Answer Key

| 1. (A) | 2. (A) | 3. (A) | 4. (C) | 5. (B) | 6. (D) | 7. (C) | 8. (A) | 9. (C) | 10. (B) |
|---|---|---|---|---|---|---|---|---|---|
| 11. (A) | 12. (D) | 13. (C) | 14. (C) | 15. (A) | 16. (B) | 17. (C) | 18. (A) | 19. (B) | 20. (A) |
| 21. (B) | 22. (A) | 23. (D) | 24. (A) | 25. (B) | 26. (A) | 27. (B) | 28. (C) | 29. (D) | 30. (C) |

1. (A)

$u = -5$ cm, $m = -4$ [when the image is real, it is inverted, m is negative]

As $m = \dfrac{-v}{u} \implies v = -mu$

$$= -(-4)(-5) = -20 \text{ cm}$$

Now, $\dfrac{1}{f} = \dfrac{1}{v} + \dfrac{1}{u} = \dfrac{1}{-20} + \dfrac{1}{-5} = \dfrac{-1-4}{20} = \dfrac{-1}{4}$

$f = -4$ cm

3. (A)

For the ray falling normally,
$$\angle i = 0° = \angle r$$

Therefore, reflected ray retraces its path

4. (C)
$$m = \frac{h_2}{h_1} = \frac{I}{O}, \quad m = 5, \quad h_2 = 20 \text{ cm}$$
$$\therefore \quad h_1 = \frac{h_2}{m} = \frac{20}{5} = 4 \text{ cm}$$

5. (B)
The image formed in a plane mirror is as far behind the mirror as the object is in front of the mirror

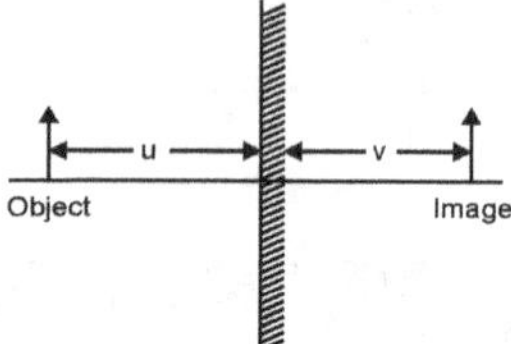


$$u = v = 10$$
Therefore, distance between object and image $u + v = 2u = 2 \times 10 = 20$ cm

6. (D)
$$m = \frac{1}{3}, \quad f = 15 \text{ cm}$$
$$m = -\frac{v}{u} = \frac{1}{3} \quad \Rightarrow \quad v = \frac{u}{3}$$
$$\text{For mirror,} \quad \frac{1}{v} + \frac{1}{u} = \frac{1}{f} \quad \Rightarrow \quad \frac{-3}{u} + \frac{1}{u} = \frac{1}{f} \quad \Rightarrow$$
$$\frac{-2}{u} + \frac{1}{f}$$
$$u = -2f$$
$$= -2 \times 15$$
$$= -30 \text{ cm}$$

7. (C)
When the object is held at $2F_1$ of convex lens, the image is formed on the other side the lens of $2F_2$ and is real and inverted.

8. (A)
$$P = P_1 + P_2 = 4 D + (-10 D) = -6 D$$

9. (C)
In case of a convex lens, the object placed at 2F from the lens forms an inverted image of the equal size at the other side of the lens at 2F distance.

10. (B)
The case is of convex lens

11. (A)
The parallel ray after refraction passes through focus on the other side of the convex lens.

12. (D)
$$u + v = 3 \text{ m (given)}$$
As maximum distance between an object and image in case of a convex lens = 4 f
$$4f = 3 \text{ m} \quad \Rightarrow \quad f = \frac{3}{4} \text{ m} = 0.75 \text{ m}$$

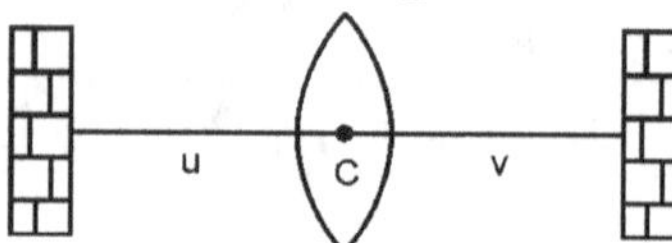


13. (C)
$$f_1 \text{ of convex lens} = 20 \text{ cm}, \quad P_1 = \frac{100}{f_1} = 5$$
D combined focal length F = 100 cm,
$$\text{combined power of } P = \frac{100}{F} = \frac{100}{100} = 1 D$$
$$P = P_1 + P_2 \quad \Rightarrow \quad P_2 \text{ (of concave lens)}$$
$$= P - P_1 = D - 5 D = -4 D$$

14. (C)
In a convex lens, when object is in front of the lens at $2F_1$, an inverted image of size of object ($h_2 = h_1$) is formed at $2F_2$. Therefore, $m = -1$.

15. (A)
$$u = -40 \text{ cm}, \quad f = -60 \text{ cm}$$
$$\frac{1}{v} - \frac{1}{u} = \frac{1}{f} \quad \Rightarrow \quad \frac{1}{v} = \frac{1}{f} + \frac{1}{u} = \frac{1}{-60} + \frac{1}{-40} = \frac{-5}{120}$$
$$v = -\frac{120}{-5} = -24 \text{ cm}$$

17. (C)
$$P = P_1 + P_2 = 1 D + (-1.5 D) = -0.5 D$$
$$P = \frac{100}{F} = -0.5 \quad \Rightarrow \quad F = -\frac{100}{0.5} = -200 \text{ cm}$$
$$= -2 m$$

18. (A)
A concave mirror producing real image is always inverted i.e., $h_2$ is negative, then m is also negative.
$$m = -3; \quad u = -10 \text{ cm};$$
$$m = \frac{-v}{u} \quad \Rightarrow \quad v = -mu = -(-3)(-10 \text{ cm})$$
$$= -30 \text{ cm}$$
Since v is also negative, image is formed in front of the mirror.

20. (A)

$f = -2\,\text{m} = -200\,\text{cm}$

$F = \dfrac{100}{f\,(\text{cm})} = \dfrac{100}{-200} - 0.5\,\text{D}$

21. (B)

When a point source is held at focus of a concave mirror or a convex lens, we get a parallel beam of light.

22. Answers can be (A) or (D) since both concave lens and prism can produce diverging rays.

23. (D)

$P = \dfrac{1}{f} \;\Rightarrow\; f = \dfrac{1}{P} = \dfrac{1}{4} = 0.25\,\text{cm}$

24. (A)

A rear view mirror used in vehicles is a convex mirror whose magnification is always less than one.

25. (B)

A full length image of a tall object can definitely be seen using a convex mirror.

29. (D)

A ray of light incident obliquely at some angle would bend the most in the liquid whose refractive index is maximum.

30. (C)

The ray of light incident on a concave mirror in a direction parallel to principal axis must pass through focus F on reflection from the mirror.

## HOTS (ACHIEVERS SECTION)

| 31. (B) | 32. (D) | 33. (D) | 34. (C) | 35. (C) |
|---|---|---|---|---|

33. (D)

virtual, erect, and diminished image

Concave mirror has the ability to produce a virtual, erect, and diminished image.

34. (C)

0 degree

Since we know $\angle i = \angle r$ for reflecting surfaces, therefore if the angle of reflection is zero, then the angle of incidence will also be zero.

35. (C)

Distance between object and image = 0.25 + 0.25 = 0.5 m

# 10. HUMAN EYE AND COLOURFUL WORLD

## Answer Key

| 1. (B) | 2. (C) | 3. (B) | 4. (A) | 5. (A) | 6. (A) | 7. (D) | 8. (B) | 9. (C) | 10. (C) |
|---|---|---|---|---|---|---|---|---|---|
| 11. (A) | 12. (D) | 13. (C) | 14. (B) | 15. (A) | 16. (B) | 17. (A) | 18. (D) | 19. (C) | 20. (C) |
| 21. (A) | 22. (C) | 23. (C) | 24. (A) | 25. (C) | 26. (B) | 27. (B) | 28. (B) | 29. (C) | 30. (A) |

9. (C)

$F = \dfrac{C}{\lambda} = \dfrac{3 \times 10^{8}\,\text{m}/\text{s}}{4000 \times 10^{-10}\,\text{m}} = 7.5 \times 10^{14}\,\text{Hz}$

12. (D)

$I_s \alpha \dfrac{1}{\lambda^4}$

13. (C)

$\dfrac{(I_s)_v}{(I_s)_r} = \left(\dfrac{\lambda_r}{\lambda_v}\right)^4 = \left(\dfrac{8000\,\text{A}°}{4000\,\text{A}°}\right)^4 = 2^4 = 16$

14. (B)

The ray of light entering a prism is refracted twice. Therefore, it bends twice on passing through the prism

16. (B)
$$n = \frac{3}{2} \qquad V_g = 3 \times 10^8 \times \frac{2}{3}$$

20. (C)

In the formation of a rainbow, the sun rays through rain drops undergo first refraction, then dispersion and finally internal reflection before coming out of the rain droplets.

21. (A)

Reddish appearance of the sun at sunrise or sunset is due to least scattering of red light.

26. (B)

A ray of light undergoes two refractions at the two faces of the prism

28. (B)

$A = 60°, \angle i = \angle e = 40°$

As $A + D = i + e \qquad \therefore \quad 60° = D = 40° + 40°$

$\Rightarrow \quad D = 80° - 60° = 20°$

## HOTS (ACHIEVERS SECTION)

| 31. (A) | 32. (B) | 33. (D) | 34. (C) | 35. (B) |
|---|---|---|---|---|

34. (C)

It is called power of accommodation of the eye.

# 11. ELECTRICITY

## Answer Key

| 1. (C) | 2. (A) | 3. (C) | 4. (A) | 5. (B) | 6. (A) | 7. (B) | 8. (B) | 9. (A) | 10. (D) |
|---|---|---|---|---|---|---|---|---|---|
| 11. (A) | 12. (B) | 13. (C) | 14. (A) | 15. (D) | 16. (C) | 17. (D) | 18. (B) | 19. (A, B) | 20. (D) |
| 21. (D) | 22. (C) | 23. (A) | 24. (D) | 25. (B) | 26. (C) | 27. (B) | 28. (A) | 29. (B) | 30. (C) |

1. (C)
$$\rho_1 = \frac{RA}{l}, \quad \rho_2 = \frac{R2A}{2l} = \frac{RA}{l} = \rho_1$$

2. (A)
Power, $P = VI = 220 \times 5 = 1100$ Watt
$P = 11 \times 100$ Watt

3. (C) $W = QV = 5 \times 10 = 50$ J

6. (A)
It is a parallel combination with two resistors each in series.
$$\frac{1}{R_e} = \frac{1}{2+2} + \frac{1}{2+2} + \frac{1}{2} = \frac{1}{4} + \frac{1}{4} = \frac{1}{2} = 1$$
$$\Rightarrow \quad R_e = 1 \, \Omega$$

8. (B)
$W = QV = 5 \times (240 - 220) = 100$ J

9. (A)
As per Ohms law, $V \propto I$

10. (D)
$$\frac{1}{R} = \frac{1}{4} + \frac{1}{4} \qquad \Rightarrow \quad R = 2 \, \Omega, \, V = 10 \text{ V}$$
$$I = \frac{V}{R} + \frac{10}{2} = 5$$

12. (B)
$R_e = 4 \, \Omega + R_p$ of 2 resistors of 6 $\Omega$ each
$$\frac{1}{R_p} = \frac{1}{6} + \frac{1}{6} \qquad \Rightarrow \quad R_p = 3 \, \Omega$$
$$\therefore \quad R_e = 4 \, \Omega + 3 \, \Omega = 7 \, \Omega$$

14. (A)
For series combination of cells, the negative terminal of first cell should be connected to the positive terminal of the second cell, and so on.

15. (D)
$I = 380 \text{ mA} = 380 \times 10{-3}\text{A}, \, V = 7.6 \text{ V}$

$$R = \frac{V}{I} = \frac{7.6\,V}{380 \times 10^{-3}\,A} = 20\,\Omega$$

**19. (A)**

The voltmeter should be connected parallel to the resistor and the ammeter should be in series with the resistor.

**23. (A)**

Slope of the graph $= \dfrac{I}{V} = \dfrac{1}{R}$, i.e., $R \propto \dfrac{1}{slope}$

Slope is the least for A, hence resistance is maximum for graph A.

**25. (B)**

When length $(l)$ of a wire doubled $(2\,l)$, its cross-sectional area $(A)$ is reduced to half $(A/2)$ as the volume of the wire is constant.

Now resistance of the wire

$$R' = \rho\,\frac{2\,l}{A/2} = 4\left(\rho\,\frac{l}{A}\right) = 4\,R$$

**26. (C)**

$V = I\,R$

$$\frac{1}{R_1} = \frac{1}{6} + \frac{1}{3} = \frac{1}{2} \quad \Rightarrow \quad R_1 = 2\,\Omega$$

$R_2 = 2\,\Omega$ (as shown)

$R_e = 2 + 2 = 4\,\Omega$

Current $I = 2\,A$

$\therefore \quad V = 2 \times 4 = 8$ volts

**27. (B)**

$$R \propto \frac{1}{A}, \quad A = \pi r^2 \text{ (cross-sectional area of a wire)}$$

**28. (A)**

$Q = I\,t = 0.5 \times (2 \times 60 \text{ min} \times 60 \text{ sec})$
$\qquad = 3600 \text{ seconds}$

**Note:** Wattage of bulb does not affect the flow of charge in this case

**30. (C)**

Resistance of each half $= \dfrac{1\,\Omega}{2} = 0.5\,\Omega$ $(R \propto l)$

Since these two halves are in parallel,

Resultant resistance $= \dfrac{R_1 \times R_2}{R_1 + R_2} = 0.25\,\Omega$

## HOTS (ACHIEVERS SECTION)

| 31. (C) | 32. (A) | 33. (B) | 34. (B) | 35. (C) |
|---|---|---|---|---|

## 12. MAGNETIC EFFECTS OF ELECTRIC CURRENT

### Answer Key

| 1. (C) | 2. (A) | 3. (B) | 4. (D) | 5. (B) | 6. (D) | 7. (B) | 8. (C) | 9. (A) | 10. (B) |
|---|---|---|---|---|---|---|---|---|---|
| 11. (A) | 12. (C) | 13. (C) | 14. (A) | 15. (D) | 16. (A) | 17. (D) | 18. (C) | 19. (B) | 20. (D) |
| 21. (D) | 22. (B) | 23. (C) | 24. (A) | 25. (D) | 26. (C) | 27. (B) | 28. (D) | 29. (A) | 30. (C) |

**3. (B)**

It has been found that Force (F) acting on a current-carrying conductor placed on a magnetic field, in a direction perpendicular to the direction of the magnetic field, is directly proportional to the current, length of the conductor and magnitude of the field

$F = k\,I\,l\,B$. In SI units, constant $k = 1$

Also, force acting on a suspended mass $= mg$

$\Rightarrow \quad mg = I\,l\,B$

$\Rightarrow \quad B = \dfrac{mg}{I\,l}$

$$= \frac{(200 \times 10^{-3}\,kg)\,(9.8\,m/s^2)}{(2\,A)\,(1.5\,m)} = 0.65\,T$$

5. **(B)**

Magnetic field $\propto \dfrac{1}{r}$

When r doubles (10 cm to 20 cm), the magnetic field becomes half (2 T → 1 T)

6. **(D)**

Magnetic field due to current-carrying wire is independent of its diameter or cross-sectional area of so long as the current remains the same.

7. **(B)**

$B \propto n\,I,\ B' = \left(\dfrac{n}{2}\right)^{1} \times 2I = nI = B$

11. **(A)**

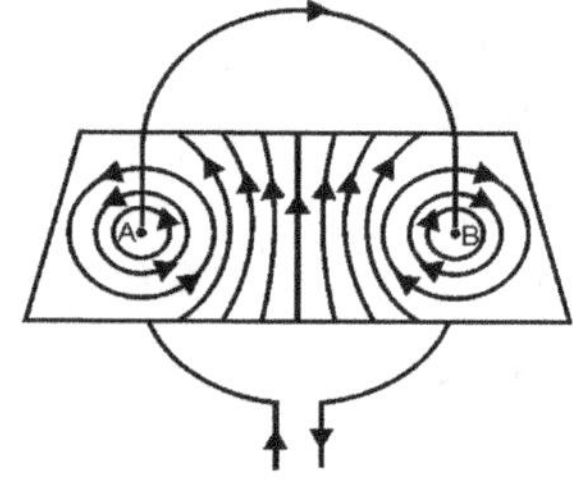

The two magnetic fields, each due to the semicircular segment of the coil through A and B, assist each other as we move towards the centre of the coil.

13. **(C)**

Fuse wire is made of an alloy of lead (75%) and tin (25%) which melts at around 200 °C.

15. **(D)**

In India the frequency of AC is 50 Hz which means that AC changes its polarity after $\dfrac{1}{100}s$ (i.e., 100 times per second) as it completes one cycle i.e., from + ve to –ve and from –ve to + ve $\dfrac{1}{50}$ sec.

17. **(D)**

Resistivity of the coil will determine the resistance of the coil and the induced current through it.

19. **(B)**

5 Hz means that the bulb glows only 5 times in a second. For the bulb to appear as glowing continuously, the frequency of AC should be at least 16 Hz.

22. **(B)**

The magnetic field for a point inside a long straight current-carrying solenoid is double than for a point situated at one of its ends.

23. **(C)**

A permanent magnet is weak

<table>
<tr><td colspan="5" align="center">HOTS (ACHIEVERS SECTION)</td></tr>
<tr><td>31. (B)</td><td>32. (D)</td><td>33. (B)</td><td>34. (C)</td><td>35. (A)</td></tr>
</table>

## 13. SOURCES OF ENERGY

### Answer Key

| 1. (D) | 2. (B) | 3. (D) | 4. (A) | 5. (B) | 6. (C) | 7. (C) | 8. (A) | 9. (D) | 10. (B) |
|---|---|---|---|---|---|---|---|---|---|
| 11. (C) | 12. (B) | 13. (A) | 14. (D) | 15. (D) | 16. (B) | 17. (C) | 18. (B) | 19. (D) | 20. (A) |
| 21. (C) | 22. (A) | 23. (D) | 24. (B) | 25. (A) | 26. (C) | 27. (A) | 28. (C) | 29. (B) | 30. (A) |

1. **(D)**

All fossil fuels like coal, oil and natural gas are non-renewable sources of energy.

2. **(B)**

Fossil fuel, hydro energy, bio energy and wind energy are conventional sources of energy. Solar energy, ocean energy (tide, wave and ocean thermal), geothermal and nuclear energy are non-conventional sources of energy.

4. **(A)**

Denmark generates 25% of its electric power requirement from wind energy.

5. **(B)**

Uranium is used as nuclear fuel is nuclear fission reaction.

6. **(C)**

Anaerobic bacteria ferment the biodegradable material such as biomass, manure, sewage, municipal waste, plant waste in the absence of oxygen to produce biogas.

7. **(C)**

Natural gas gives off 50% of the $CO_2$ released by coal and 25% less $CO_2$ than oil for the same amount of energy produced.

8. **(A)**

Yes, if we plant trees in a planned manner to ensure a continuous supply of wood.

16. **(B)**

Petroleum on fractional distillation yields diesel, kerosene, petrol or gasoline, petroleum gas, asphalt, lubricating oil, paraffin wax.

18. **(B)**

Suitable technologies are being developed to overcome difficulties in the way of using hydrogen as a fuel in near future.

21. **(C)**

Coke LPG are secondary fuels whereas wood and petroleum are primary fuels.

22. **(A)**

Solar cell is made of silicon which is a good semiconductor.

24. **(B)**

Wind power, $P = \pi r^2 \rho v^3$, where, v is the speed and $\rho$ is density of air.

## 14. OUR ENVIRONMENT

### Answer Key

| 1. (D) | 2. (C) | 3. (C) | 4. (A) | 5. (D) | 6. (C) | 7. (B) | 8. (D) | 9. (A) | 10. (D) |
|---|---|---|---|---|---|---|---|---|---|
| 11. (D) | 12. (D) | 13. (A) | 14. (C) | 15. (B) | 16. (B) | 17. (B) | 18. (C) | 19. (B) | 20. (A) |
| 21. (D) | 22. (D) | 23. (B) | 24. (C) | 25. (C) | 26. (D) | 27. (A) | 28. (B) | 29. (B) | 30. (C) |

### HOTS (ACHIEVERS SECTION)

| 31. (A) | 32. (D) | 33. (D) | 34. (B) | 35. (B) |
|---|---|---|---|---|

## 15. LOGICAL REASONING

### Answer Key

| 1. (C) | 2. (B) | 3. (A) | 4. (B) | 5. (D) | 6. (A) | 7. (C) | 8. (A) | 9. (D) | 10. (B) |
|---|---|---|---|---|---|---|---|---|---|
| 11. (A) | 12. (C) | 13. (D) | 14. (C) | 15. (C) | 16. (A) | 17. (D) | 18. (C) | 19. (B) | 20. (D) |
| 21. (A) | 22. (C) | 23. (D) | 24. (A) | 25. (E) | 26. (C) | 27. (C) | 28. (D) | 29. (B) | 30. (B) |
| 31. (B) | 32. (D) | 33. (C) | 34. (D) | 35. (C) | 36. (D) | | | | |

1. **(C)**

$2836 = 2 + 8 - 3 + 6 = 13$

$9423 = 9 + 4 - 2 + 3 = 14$

$7229 = 7 + 2 - 2 + 9 = 16$

2. **(B)**

$$211 \Rightarrow 2 + 1 + 1 = 4$$
$$333 \Rightarrow 3 + 3 + 3 = 9 \Big] + 5$$

Similarly

$$356 \Rightarrow 3+5+6 = 14$$
$$388 \Rightarrow 3+8+8 = 19$$
$$\Big\} +5$$

3. (A)

TSR : FED :: WVU : MLK
$\overleftarrow{\phantom{TSR}}$ $\overleftarrow{\phantom{FED}}$ $\overleftarrow{\phantom{WVU}}$

4. (B)

Except whale, all are reptiles.

5. (D)

Except ornament, all are different kinds of ornaments.

6. (A)

All others are continents.

7. (C)

Here

|   | C | O | M | E |
|---|---|---|---|---|
|   | $-1\downarrow$ | $-1\downarrow$ | $-1\downarrow$ | $-1\downarrow$ |
|   | B | N | L | D |

Then

|   | B | R | I | N | G |
|---|---|---|---|---|---|
| $\Rightarrow$ | $\downarrow-1$ | $\downarrow-1$ | $\downarrow-1$ | $\downarrow-1$ | $\downarrow-1$ |
|   | A | Q | H | M | F |

8. (A)

By reversing the order

Here      SILVER → REVLIS

Similarly   BLACK → KCALB

9. (D)

Given

| R | O | P | E |   | A | P | P | L | E |
|---|---|---|---|---|---|---|---|---|---|
| $\downarrow$ | $\downarrow$ | $\downarrow$ | $\downarrow$ |   | $\downarrow$ | $\downarrow$ | $\downarrow$ | $\downarrow$ | $\downarrow$ |
| 3 | 4 | 5 | 6 |   | 1 | 5 | 5 | 2 | 6 |

then Direct substitution

$5 \to P$ $4 \to O$ $6 \to E$ $1 \to A$ $3 \to R$

Hence 54613 → POEAR

10. (B)

7th day of a month is three days earlier than Friday that is Tuesday

14th day is Tuesday

19th day is Sunday.

11. (A)

Given P is 18th from the front. R is 24th

Number of persons between P and R = 6

R is exactly in the middle of P and Q.

and no. of persons between R and Q = 6

Hence $\xleftrightarrow{\;17\;} P \xleftrightarrow{\;6\;} R \xleftrightarrow{\;6\;} Q \xleftrightarrow{\;15\;}$

number of persons in the queue

= 17 + 1 + 6 + 1 + 6 + 1 + 15 = 47

12. (C)

On subtracting 3 from the middle digit the numbers become

559, 332, 524, 341, 412

Now reversing the positions of digits,

955, 233, 425, 143, 214

Arranging the above numbers in descending order, we get

955, 425, (233), 214, 143

↑ Middle No.

Hence 3 is required number.

13. (D)

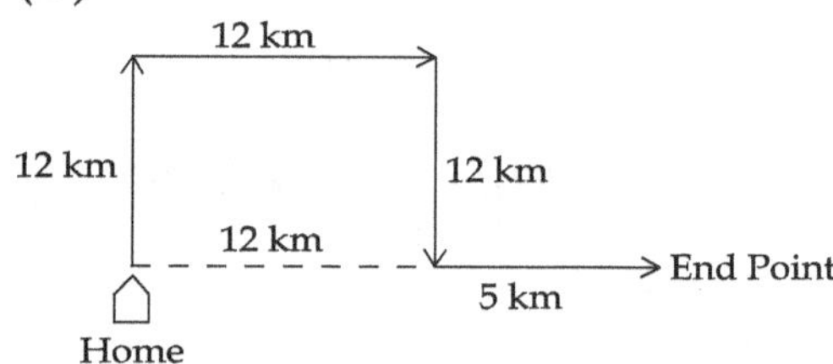


Distance = 12 + 5 = 17 km in east direction

14. (C)

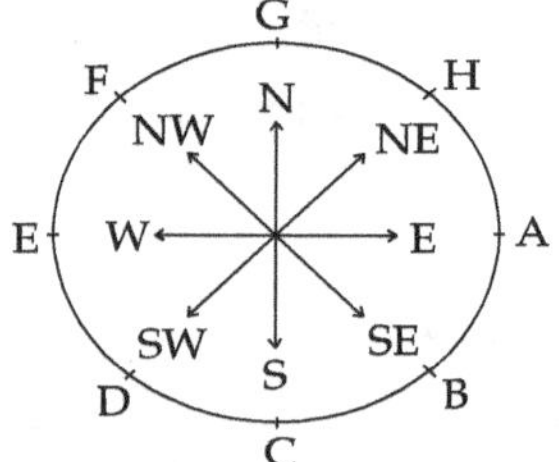


Position of D is in south-west.

15. (C)

The movement of Dinesh is as given below.

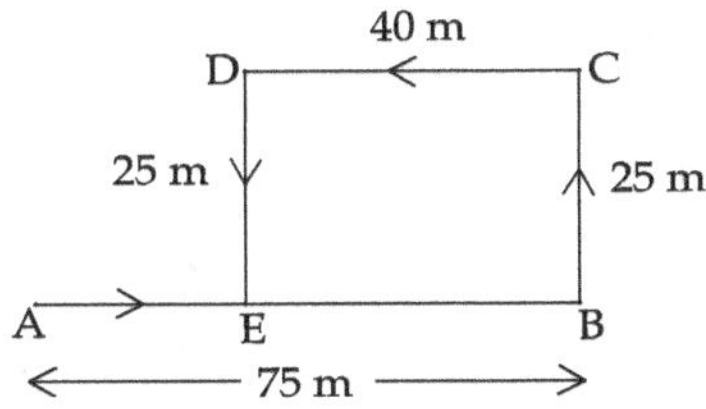

From above fig. EB = DC = 40m

Dinesh's distance from the starting point A

= AE = AB - EB

= 75 - 40 = 35 m

16. (A)

E is not present in the given word.

17. (D)

There is only one E in the given word.

18. (C)

N is not present in the given word.

19. (B)

Punam's mother Mamta is the youngest sister of Mishra and sister of Prabhat. Prabhat is Punam's uncle.

20. (D)

Only son of Rekha's grandmother means Rekha's father and his son is Rekha's brother.

21. (A)

Daughter of grandmother = Aunt.

Aunt's only brother = Father

22. (C)

Given 20 - 10 = 200

but 20 × 10 = 200; - stands for ×.

Given 8 ÷ 4 = 12 but 8 + 4 = 12

∴ ÷ stands for +

Given 6 × 2 = 4 but 6 - 2 = 4

∴ × stands for -

Given expression

$= 100 - 10 × 1000 ÷ 1000 + 100 × 10$

$= 100 × 10 - 1000 + 1000 ÷ 100 - 10$

$= 1000 - 1000 + 1000 ÷ 100 - 10$

$= 1000 - 1000 + 10 - 10$

$= 0 + 0 = 0$

23. (D)

We have (10 C 4) A (4 C 4) B 6

$= (10 × 4) + (4 × 4) - 6 = 40 + 16 - 6 = 50$

24. (A)

Using correct symbols, we have

$(3 × 15 + 19) ÷ 8 - 6$

$= (45 + 19) ÷ 8 - 6$

$= 64 ÷ 8 - 6 = 8 - 6 = 2$

25. (E)

The circle moves sequentially one, two, three, four, ...... spaces (each space is equal to half-a-side of the square boundary) in an ACW direction.

26. (C)

The number of sides of the figure reduces by one in each step.

27. (C)

Vertical and horizontal line segments are added to the figure alternately.

## MODEL TEST PAPER

### Answer Key

| 1. (B) | 2. (C) | 3. (A) | 4. (C) | 5. (C) | 6. (B) | 7. (C) | 8. (A) | 9. (C) | 10. (B) |
|---|---|---|---|---|---|---|---|---|---|
| 11. (A) | 12. (C) | 13. (A) | 14. (A) | 15. (B) | 16. (A) | 17. (C) | 18. (C) | 19. (D) | 20. (C) |
| 21. (A) | 22. (A) | 23. (C) | 24. (A) | 25. (C) | 26. (B) | 27. (A) | 28. (C) | 29. (B) | 30. (D) |
| 31. (A) | 32. (A) | 33. (C) | 34. (A) | 35. (A) | 36. (B) | 37. (C) | 38. (A) | 39. (C) | 40. (A) |
| 41. (B) | 42. (B) | 43. (A) | 44. (A) | 45. (B) | 46. (B) | 47. (C) | 48. (D) | 49. (A) | 50. (A) |

# SAMPLE OMR ANSWER SHEET

## 1. STUDENT NAME (IN ENGLISH CAPITAL LETTERS ONLY)

Students must write and darken the respective circles completely using HB Pencil only. Othewise their Answer Sheets will not be evaluated.

## PERSONAL DETAILS

### 2. SCHOOL CODE

### 3. CLASS

### 4. SECTION

### 5. ROLL NO.

### 6. QUESTION PAPER SET

A ○
B ○
C ○
D ○

### 7. MOBILE NUMBER

### 8. GENDER

MALE ○

FEMALE ○

### 9. STREAM
(Only for Class XI and XII Students)

MATHEMATICS ○
BIOLOGY ○
OTHERS ○

## MARK YOUR ANSWERS

| 1. | Ⓐ Ⓑ Ⓒ Ⓓ | 26. | Ⓐ Ⓑ Ⓒ Ⓓ |
| 2. | Ⓐ Ⓑ Ⓒ Ⓓ | 27. | Ⓐ Ⓑ Ⓒ Ⓓ |
| 3. | Ⓐ Ⓑ Ⓒ Ⓓ | 28. | Ⓐ Ⓑ Ⓒ Ⓓ |
| 4. | Ⓐ Ⓑ Ⓒ Ⓓ | 29. | Ⓐ Ⓑ Ⓒ Ⓓ |
| 5. | Ⓐ Ⓑ Ⓒ Ⓓ | 30. | Ⓐ Ⓑ Ⓒ Ⓓ |
| 6. | Ⓐ Ⓑ Ⓒ Ⓓ | 31. | Ⓐ Ⓑ Ⓒ Ⓓ |
| 7. | Ⓐ Ⓑ Ⓒ Ⓓ | 32. | Ⓐ Ⓑ Ⓒ Ⓓ |
| 8. | Ⓐ Ⓑ Ⓒ Ⓓ | 33. | Ⓐ Ⓑ Ⓒ Ⓓ |
| 9. | Ⓐ Ⓑ Ⓒ Ⓓ | 34. | Ⓐ Ⓑ Ⓒ Ⓓ |
| 10. | Ⓐ Ⓑ Ⓒ Ⓓ | 35. | Ⓐ Ⓑ Ⓒ Ⓓ |
| 11. | Ⓐ Ⓑ Ⓒ Ⓓ | 36. | Ⓐ Ⓑ Ⓒ Ⓓ |
| 12. | Ⓐ Ⓑ Ⓒ Ⓓ | 37. | Ⓐ Ⓑ Ⓒ Ⓓ |
| 13. | Ⓐ Ⓑ Ⓒ Ⓓ | 38. | Ⓐ Ⓑ Ⓒ Ⓓ |
| 14. | Ⓐ Ⓑ Ⓒ Ⓓ | 39. | Ⓐ Ⓑ Ⓒ Ⓓ |
| 15. | Ⓐ Ⓑ Ⓒ Ⓓ | 40. | Ⓐ Ⓑ Ⓒ Ⓓ |
| 16. | Ⓐ Ⓑ Ⓒ Ⓓ | 41. | Ⓐ Ⓑ Ⓒ Ⓓ |
| 17. | Ⓐ Ⓑ Ⓒ Ⓓ | 42. | Ⓐ Ⓑ Ⓒ Ⓓ |
| 18. | Ⓐ Ⓑ Ⓒ Ⓓ | 43. | Ⓐ Ⓑ Ⓒ Ⓓ |
| 19. | Ⓐ Ⓑ Ⓒ Ⓓ | 44. | Ⓐ Ⓑ Ⓒ Ⓓ |
| 20. | Ⓐ Ⓑ Ⓒ Ⓓ | 45. | Ⓐ Ⓑ Ⓒ Ⓓ |
| 21. | Ⓐ Ⓑ Ⓒ Ⓓ | 46. | Ⓐ Ⓑ Ⓒ Ⓓ |
| 22. | Ⓐ Ⓑ Ⓒ Ⓓ | 47. | Ⓐ Ⓑ Ⓒ Ⓓ |
| 23. | Ⓐ Ⓑ Ⓒ Ⓓ | 48. | Ⓐ Ⓑ Ⓒ Ⓓ |
| 24. | Ⓐ Ⓑ Ⓒ Ⓓ | 49. | Ⓐ Ⓑ Ⓒ Ⓓ |
| 25. | Ⓐ Ⓑ Ⓒ Ⓓ | 50. | Ⓐ Ⓑ Ⓒ Ⓓ |

Signature of the Student & Date of Examination

Signature of the Invigilator & Date of Examination

V&S Publishers, F-2/16 Ansari Road, Daryaganj, New Delhi-110002, ☎ 011-23240026-27
✉ info@vspublishers.com, ⊕ www.vspublishers.com